I hope this book helps to open your heart and let your life shine. Cheri ♡

A MESSAGE FROM St. FRANCIS

An Ancient Mystic Speaks To The Modern World

As channeled by

Cheri Harris

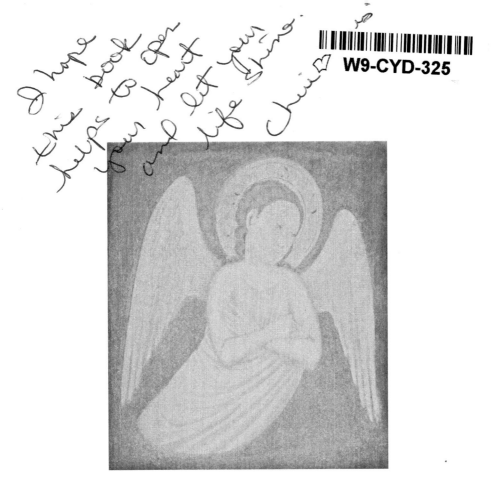

SUMMERLAND
PUBLISHING

Third Edition: May 2007
ISBN: 978-0-9794585-5-2

Photographs by Cheri Harris.

Cover:
Giotto's School, 14th c., San Damiano Sanctuary, Assisi

"Road to La Verna From Assisi" map used by permission of Father Fiorenzo Locatelli, Prior of the Monastery of La Verna.

Printed in the U. S. A.

Library of Congress Control Number: 2006932819

Table of Contents

Messages From St. Francis

Dedication

This book is dedicated to my caring and compassionate Dad. Although you have gone on to another realm, I feel your loving presence and guidance all around me, stronger than ever.

You are my sweet angel.

With Appreciation To

My dear sister Debbie, for always being there for me throughout my life. Thanks for being such an incredible support while this book was being written. Your encouragement and belief in my relationship with St. Francis helped me to trust in myself, so I could be a willing voice through which St. Francis could transmit his book;

Konstanz Kuraz, for her gift of love. Thanks for your immense participation, both for your suggestions and proof reading to help complete the book. You did a superb job;

Terry Favour, for her caring. Thanks for your feedback on the book;

My brother and sister-in-law Craig and Giselle, for their patience. Thanks for hosting me while I was in the States working on the book;

My parents Mary and Art, for their constant love and support. Thanks for providing a childhood that gave me the opportunity to comfortably seek to explore the depths of my soul;

My dear husband Ago, for his love, strength, passion, and dedication to our relationship. Thanks for the many long hours of help on the computer to get this book ready. Thanks also, for bringing me to Italy, which was the stepping stone that started my relationship with St. Francis. You are what keeps the fire burning in my heart;

My mentor St. Francis, for giving me the opportunity to feel his all-encompassing loving energy, throughout my body and soul. Thanks for your total dedication to Simplicity, Compassion, Mother Nature, Peace, and Love, which has kept you in the forefront after eight hundred years as one of the most important mystics of all times. Your presence is so alive in the hearts of millions because of your accessibility and strong desire to help each and every one of us to become better people and to understand the truth of our existence. I love you for that. You are my friend and my guiding light.

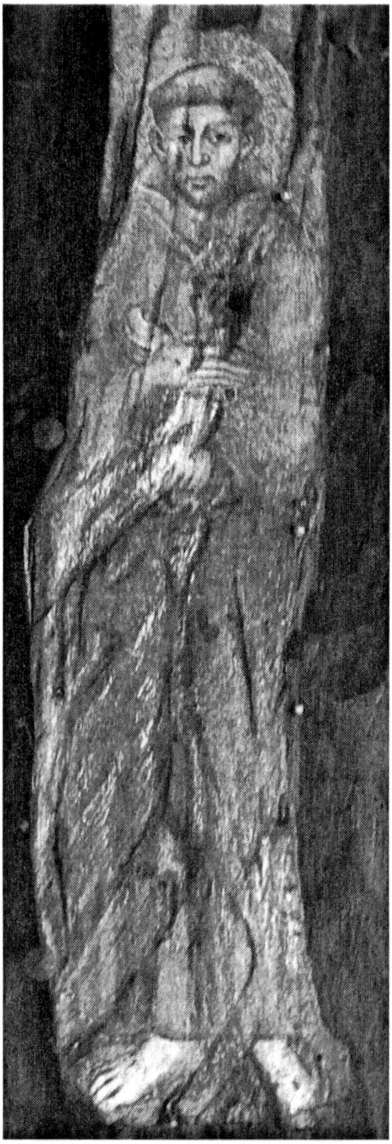

Copy of St. Francis by Cimabue (1280 ca.)
The Hermitage – Assisi

Simple Prayer of St. Francis

Lord, make me an instrument of your peace.
Where there is hatred, let me sow love.
Where there is injury, pardon.

Where there is discord, unity.
Where there is doubt, faith.

Where there is error, truth.
Where there is despair, hope.
Where there is sadness, joy.

Where there is darkness, light.

O Divine Master, grant that I may not so much seek
to be consoled, as to console;
to be understood, as to understand;
to be loved, as to love.
For it is in giving, that we receive.
It is in pardoning, that we are pardoned.
It is in dying, that we are born to eternal life.

Preface

A decade ago, I visited a psychic who told me I would be writing a book in about ten years. I was shocked at this prediction, not believing that I had the desire or the capability to write. However, this prediction ultimately proved to be true when I began channeling information from St. Francis and, following his instructions, wrote this book to share his insights with others.

When you channel, the information comes through you, not from you, which makes a difference in the writing process. To channel, all you need is trust that you truly are being contacted by a wise soul that's not in a physical body, along with the ability to listen with intense concentration to what's being said so that you can record it as clearly as possible. The energy flowing into me from this beautiful being is what confirmed for me that I was genuinely receiving these messages from St. Francis and not simply "making it up." St. Francis's distinct presence and his unique style of communicating ideas always instilled a peace inside me that made everything in the world seem okay.

The first question most people ask is, "Why did St. Francis choose you?" Allow me to delve into my past a little, to answer this as completely as possible.

As a child, my experience with religion was not very deep. I went to a Baptist Sunday school, but never felt a connection to what I was being taught. Since I was obliged to go, I made it a social affair rather than a religious experience. When I was twelve, we moved to a new house and I stopped going to church.

I had an extraordinary spiritual experience at age fifteen that opened my mind to a different reality. During this experience, I felt a complete sense of *oneness* with God and the world. After this, my perception of the world shifted and I began studying Eastern religions. I started reading books about meditation, Buddhism, yoga, and travel. I was enticed with other cultures and decided at age eighteen to travel the world. While I was traveling, I continued reading spiritual books and also attended numerous self-help and spiritual seminars that I came across.

My first contact with a "spirit" came in my early thirties when a friend and I attended a séance in San Francisco. After the group asked for an evolved spirit to contact them, one who called herself Iaya came through. Each person asked a question pertaining to areas of concern in their lives and Iaya answered by moving a glass around on a table. I was skeptical about the authenticity of this spirit, so I asked for a confirmation that she was, in fact, moving the glass. To my astonishment, seconds after my request, my eyes started twitching uncontrollably for about a minute. Each time the twitching stopped, I repeated the request. And each time I repeated the request, the same eye movements occurred.

After that, Iaya's spirit has always been with me, helping me to make difficult decisions in my life. I view her as my guardian angel and I receive her information whenever I call her, sometimes even when I don't call her. She always helps me to see things more clearly. Her method of communication is twitching my eyes: two twitches for yes and five for no. I rarely contact Iaya these days. Occasionally she appears, though, usually when I need guidance.

Another profound spiritual experience took place when I was living in Bali, Indonesia. I had just returned from a trip to a remote island, near Bali, named Flores. I was very sick and a medical report verified that I had contracted both malaria and typhoid. The doctor wanted to put me in a hospital, but I'd heard many stories about the lack of hygiene and the ineptness of the staff. I felt desperate and frightened, afraid that I might die.

That night I prayed with all my heart to Jesus. I had just read *The Teachings of the Great Masters* and I believed in his great healing powers as expressed in that book. In prayer, I promised that I would help mankind if Jesus would help heal my body.

Jesus appeared in the middle of the night with a group of followers, all of whom encircled my body and laid their hands on me—Jesus put his hands around my head and face. A golden light surrounded me and I was bathed in a feeling of deep tranquility and love. Following this remarkable encounter, I recovered very quickly without having to go to the hospital. When Jesus answered my plea that night, it solidified my existing desire to help mankind, which eventually led me to my work with St. Francis.

When I once asked St. Francis why he chose me to write his book he answered, "Because of your courage and your openness. I knew you wouldn't let me down. It is too important for you to see this planet and everyone on it evolve. Actually, it was your choice to help me. I simply agreed to accept your help."

Then I asked him if we had known each other in the past. "Yes, we have spent time together. There is a bond that holds our energy together—but I have that with many, as you may well expect. It was more of your doing than mine. You want, with all your heart, to make a difference in this lifetime and to help elevate the consciousness of mankind. Now is your time to do this. Remember: it is your purpose for being here. Your petals are opening; let the sweet fragrance out. You must stop limiting yourself so that you may fully blossom into a magnificent flower, sharing the truths and beauty of existence. The sooner these messages are transmitted to others, the sooner there will be transformation."

I definitely wasn't expecting that answer. Or perhaps it is more accurate for me to say that my ego didn't like that answer. I guess I wanted to hear that I was so special and wonderful that there wasn't anyone as perfect as me to help this great saint. Of course, he put me in my place as he always does, so honestly and gently.

The second question that people usually ask is, "How do these spirits come to you?" These spirits do not appear to me physically as human beings. Rather, I see their faces in my mind, feel their presence, and hear their messages.

My actual friendship with St. Francis began in Assisi, on the Saturday before Easter in 1996. In 1990, I had moved from Bali to Italy to be with the man I love and to explore my roots, since my mother's parents came from there. Twenty years earlier, while traveling through Europe, I had spent a week in Assisi and had been struck by its beauty and tranquility. The special energy I felt enticed me to stay longer than I had planned. And now I was back, drawn by an even stronger energy than before. Assisi is considered to be a very spiritual place where many people feel the consoling and uplifting presence of St. Francis. During the weekend before Easter, I went with my husband to help him sell antiques at a market in Arezzo, about ninety minutes north of Assisi. It was a bad day for me and I can remember crying in frustration. I am a massage therapist and I was frustrated because my Italian clients wanted to be "fixed" without taking any responsibility for their own bodies. That night, I awoke with a voice in my mind saying, "Go to Assisi."

Because I usually listen to my intuition, I headed to Assisi the next day although I had no idea why I was being called there. When I arrived, I went to the hermitage where St. Francis used to meditate in the local caves. It is a beautiful location with trees and birds and is situated away from the tourist areas. I began walking along the dirt path there to the wooden cross where St. Francis gave sermons in the thirteenth century. As I walked, there appeared in my mind the image of a man with a round face and a big nose. I knew intuitively it was St. Francis because of his loving energy and appearance, wearing a brown burlap tunic with a rope as his belt.

Like a fairy tale or a dream, he began to converse with me as he mentally walked me under a rainbow toward a stone well. At the well, he sprinkled water on my head. Above me, I saw two hands in a praying position with white light around them. I then sat with him for six hours in the cold. During this time, he confirmed for me that he was really St. Francis. He took me to another realm where the feeling of love was overwhelming and he talked to me about his truths. But his main objective that day was to console me after the frustration I had felt the night before. I finally left, deeply moved from this experience. I promised St. Francis that I would return in one month. As I drove back in the car, it already seemed like a dream.

When I arrived back in Arezzo, my husband asked me how my day was and I said, "I just spent the day with St. Francis." That is how it all began! I went back a month later, as I had promised, with a pen and a notebook in hand to record what St. Francis communicated to me. This began a profound friendship as well as the manuscript for this book. I visited St. Francis one day a month in Assisi, which was a loving ritual in my life. I would ask him personal and spiritual questions to which he would reply with sound advice, in his honest and humorous way.

Then one day I discovered La Verna, a mountain village and national park. It is the place where St. Francis received his stigmata. There is a beautiful Franciscan sanctuary built on the rocks of a mountain ledge. It's a lovely place and much closer to Arezzo, so I was able to visit more frequently.

One day while I was in Assisi, St. Francis gave me a title called "Silence." When thoughts started rapidly coming to me, I jotted them down under this title. "Silence" marked the beginning of the messages that make up this book. Because St. Francis had already informed me that I was to be his messenger for this book, this new process of structuring the messages under the title he gave me came as no surprise. These messages came out of his deep concern and sincere obligation to help mankind evolve as easily and naturally as possible. He has always been a humble saint, sharing his ideas in an uncomplicated way that is accessible to ordinary people. The beauty of his teachings is that they come straight from his heart—his open, loving heart.

His main theme, and one that he repeats over and over, is the importance and urgency of *living with an open heart.* This was made profoundly clear to me when, shortly after we met, I sat with him among the trees and birds while he beamed a pink laser light from his heart to mine, connecting our hearts together. My own heart started pounding so hard and fast that I felt as if I was going to have a heart attack. Then I felt my heart unblocking, allowing new openness and vulnerability to shine through. It was a feeling of excitement and deep love that lasted the whole day. I realized that he had, in effect, charged my heart vibrationally with his laser of love.

Today, I know that every time I sit in silence, he will be there reminding me to reclaim that same sensation and to intentionally and consciously open my heart so that the love can pour out. Yet, even with all his help, it's not always easy for me. This speaks to me of its tremendous importance because it is, in fact, the only thing that St. Francis has insisted that I work on.

Finally, I want to share with you how my relationship with St. Francis and the writing of this book have greatly affected my life. I have tried to keep my life as normal as possible. For the first year or so of our contact, I told very few people about my friendship with St. Francis, fearing that their reactions would keep me from speaking about this experience and that my life would change dramatically. Such fears, undoubtedly, impeded me from moving forward. But I realize that now is the time for me to come out into the open and reveal the wisdom I have channeled from St. Francis.

I look upon my relationship with St. Francis as a deep friendship. Yes, he is my teacher, but he always treats me like an equal whose thoughts and ideas are as valid as his. One day when I was angry with him for not coming to my aid, he clearly, but gently, let me know that I am in control of my own life and that he would not, and could not, interfere.

Although I realize that I haven't completely opened myself to the teachings of St. Francis, and that I still have a fear of death—the biggest illusion of all—I look forward to the day when such fears will disappear and I will be free. In the meantime, I will faithfully reveal the messages that St. Francis wants so much for me to bring to all people who are interested.

St. Francis is my guru. He is my master. But most of all, he is my friend—and this is a fact that I will cherish for eternity.

Cheri

Author's Note from St. Francis

Dear beloved souls, there are many of you out there that feel very close to me and what I represented in the past. I appreciate this, immensely, and thank you for all your support. I want to say that my life as St. Francis was a beautiful life, and still is. The difference now, however, is that I am not limited to a body. My consciousness is ever moving and changing. The beliefs and ideas I held onto so strongly in the past have been *uprooted* so that a higher awareness could arise. All of us must move and transcend thought patterns that no longer serve us. I, too, am constantly transforming. Just because I no longer have a body doesn't mean I am stuck at the place where I was when my body died. What help would that do? It only perpetuates past concepts that no longer apply today, in our present world.

I am now living with you, in the moment, and have transformed some of my old beliefs. For example, in the past I chose a life of great suffering. It was what I needed for my soul to evolve at that time. However, that doesn't mean that I would choose, or need, that same path today. I now see the greater picture, a picture in which one can also become aware without the aid of suffering. The beauty is that there are so many different paths to choose from. This may defy all that I stood for in the past, but who wants to be labeled as something so concrete that there is no room for change? The messages in this book reflect how I see things now, naturally, not how I saw them when I was alive in the thirteenth century.

My soul is living as a blade of grass, rustling from side to side in the wind. I don't care which direction it moves. I let nature make that choice.

St. Francis Basilica - Assisi

Road to La Verna From Assisi

A Message From St. Francis

Messages From St. Francis

Art by Marika Arena

A Message From St. Francis

Becoming as Free as a Bird

In western societies we are allowed a wide spectrum of choice in making life's decisions. Like birds, our boundaries can be unlimited. We may soar to the heavens and beyond because our freedom can manifest in any form we choose. The variations of self-expression are vast, and to experiment with this vastness is what we are here for. It's not the outcome that matters, but the journey through experience itself that is important.

Living in a free society may allow for greater experimentation with self-expression, but if the mind is imprisoned, no physical place can liberate us no matter how "free" it is. That is why we must concentrate on freeing the mind from preconceived ideas and archaic belief systems that keep us trapped.

Because most of us are creatures of habit, it is easy to unconsciously choose ideas that imprison rather than liberate us. Our fears are so great that they control how we think and behave. Becoming conscious and expanding our awareness is the key to transcending these fears and false beliefs. This is not an easy task because we have become comfortable with these beliefs and the mind does not want to let them go. These false beliefs are like the sound of a scratched record repeating over and over what has become ingrained.

The way to freedom is opened by understanding that we are not our mind or our thoughts. Our hearts are naturally open, but it's thoughts that create paranoia and close the heart. The trust we have in the mind (thoughts) has continually worked against us. The mind is not a trustworthy friend, but instead constantly deceives us. If we truly realized this, we would not rely on the mind for truth. It's our soul's awareness that is connected to all truth and this is what we must reunite with. We must let our soul guide our thoughts and actions, which will then free the mind of its antiquated belief systems.

What must we do to create this reunion with our soul? First, we must realize that the soul is our link to God and the essence of who we are. It is never born and never dies, but is eternal. Our soul has the same qualities as God. Most of us have lost the awareness of this because we believe that we are the mind rather than the soul. Consciousness is waiting for us to realize our true nature. Unlike the mind, it will not force anything upon us. Instead, it waits for us to take the first step.

The soul is the foundation of who we are, not the mind. The deeper we go within, and the more silent we become, the easier it is to feel and know our "soul essence," which is one with God. We may connect with our soul through many different techniques and qualities, such as: meditation, contemplation, prayer, silence, dreams, therapy, opening the heart, bodywork, love, service, compassion, generosity, and honesty.

We must diligently work to incorporate all of these techniques and qualities into our daily lives. We cannot allow laziness, indifference, or fear to deter our commitment. We cannot let wrongdoings from the past, reluctance in the present, or false expectations for the future discourage us. Our hearts and souls want us to rediscover who we really are. Aren't you curious to know your true being?

I invite you to know yourself and to love yourself. For eventually, no matter how many lives we might live, we will learn to know, like I do, the incredible, beautiful, perfect, and free beings that we truly are.

Opening the Heart

The heart is the basis of our physical and emotional life. One of its many functions is to keep our bodies pulsating with life's force. The heart is also a great transmitter of emotions. It transmits the many feelings we have to the body for physical expression, thus creating union between our physical and emotional aspects of being.

The heart is the part of the body where our truth lies. It is the center and the core of all human feelings. This truth cannot be seen or measured by science. Unfortunately, this lack of scientific proof has minimized the significance of this all-empowering organ in our present day cultures. We all know that the heart keeps us alive physically with every beat it makes. But in reality, it's so much more than this. On an emotional level, when we are feeling either pain or love, we see it as coming from the heart. The heart is wide open when it feels love and it is constricted and closed when it feels pain.

In our culture, we place much importance on the physical aspects of the heart. Because of scientific testing, we know that the heart works better with special diets and exercise. Consequently, there are hundreds of programs promising a longer life and a healthier heart if we take this pill or follow that diet. But the heart is so much greater than this. It's not just another organ to be exploited for financial gain. We have lost our relationship with our heart by not valuing it as we should. It is sacred and holy and is our connection to God. The heart must be treated with the love and respect that it deserves.

Many times, we close our hearts because we are afraid to feel pain, sorrow, despair, and emptiness. What we don't realize is that by doing this we are also shutting out all the goodness that prevails within us. For without pain, how would we know joy? And without hate, how would we know love? Without the negative feelings, the positive feelings could not exist either. We must see that each feeling has its opposite mate, and when we invite one in, room is also made for the other. So in order to feel love, we must have already felt hate. If the two opposite feelings are felt and truly accepted, they lose their hold on us. This allows us to focus our attention on the truth of who we are rather than to focus on our dualistic feelings.

So, let's open our hearts and let all the feelings in—the beautiful and the ugly. When our hearts are completely open, we can feel every variety of love that has ever existed. And in that love, we will learn to accept hate. Love always overrides negativity; its force is so powerful that it can transform us from being a fearful person into a loving and accepting person, from being a self-centered person into a compassionate person, and from being a person who feels separate into a person who feels whole. Having an open heart can transform us internally into a complete person who is full of beauty.

We all know what it is like to feel alone in the midst of a crowd of people. Unfortunately, other people cannot give us the sense of union we are searching for—we are the only ones who can. We accomplish this by being true to ourselves and by allowing our hearts—rather than our heads—to communicate our honest feelings to others. The heart's main purpose is to enable us to feel the love that we actually are and then to outwardly express that love in our lives. This is impossible to do when our hearts are closed. So our work on this planet is to keep our hearts more and more open.

The more we are consumed by the mind, the harder this is to do. Realizing this, we must learn to address all of our feelings, good and bad, so that we may remain whole and in our total truth. When we address only a part of ourselves instead of the whole of ourselves, we feel separate and alone, thus creating a sense of depression and alienation from ourselves and others. Your heart is your savior! So you must use your heart to its fullest. When you do this, your life will blossom and be renewed. Every petal of your True Self will be able to merge together to make one beautiful and complete flower. And this flower will represent you as a whole universe unto itself.

You may ask yourself, "Who am I really?" Sit quietly with this question and bathe in it, for it is a very important question and one that will greatly affect your choices in life. Let these choices be made from the depths of your own vibrating heart, for only then can you be sure that they come from truth. This truth is meant to be manifested here and now. It's not just for the totality of your own soul, but for the totality of *all* souls. For when your heart has felt this truth profoundly, all other souls will benefit as well. And their hearts, too, will open. And this unison of joy will permeate throughout the universe.

Your heart dictates to you. You are its owner, so treat it with kindness and be good to it. You alone hold the key to unlock the door to your heart; therefore you, and only you, can open your heart. Only in your heart will you find what you've always been searching for. Let that search be finished, because you have found the key to what you have been looking for—the truth of your being.

The following visualization will help you open your heart and experience more joy in your life. This visualization is most beneficial when taped and then stopped at the places where your emotions are being felt.

Close your eyes and put your attention on your heart. Visualize your heart. Notice that there is a doorknob in the middle of it. At this moment, an angel appears and says, "Here is the key that will unlock and open the door to your heart." You take the key and unlock the door. When you open the door, you see another door with a lock.

At this moment, another angel comes to you and hands you a key. She says, "This key will unlock the door." You put the key in the lock. The door unlocks, but it is difficult to open. At first, you feel a little scared because you don't know what's behind the door. But the angel smiles and says, "It's okay, open the door." You push the door open. It's getting darker and harder to see, but you are able to see another doorknob.

Now another angel appears, hands you a key, and says, "Open the door, don't be afraid." The fear you have this time is stronger, and it envelops your whole body. You become paralyzed and cannot move. You then ask yourself, "What is this fear that is so strong in me that I'm so afraid to open this door?" Emotions start to pour out. Could it be fear of the unknown? Could it be fear of death, fear of pain, or fear of rejection? Go inside for a moment and ask yourself, "What is it that I truly fear?"

Then you hear an angel's voice saying, "Open the door, don't be afraid." You feel a sensation that if you don't open the door now these fears will take over and you will be controlled by them the rest of your life. So you take the key and unlock the door, but the door is too heavy to open. You push, but it doesn't move.

You hear a voice deep inside of you that says, "Have no fear, I am here, and I will give you the strength to open the door." You know with your deepest intuition that your soul, your true essence, is speaking to you. You put your hand on the doorknob, you turn it, and now the door moves easily. You slowly open it and a piercing gold light appears.

As you walk into the light, a strong feeling of love encompasses you. Feel the love; it is so strong that you could burst. Go into the love. Notice that your heart is pounding fast. Then ask yourself, "Is this what it means to have an open heart, full of love and compassion? How can I always feel like this?" Just remember to keep the doors always open. And if they do happen to close, just use the keys that you now know you always possess.

Silence

Silence is what quiets the mind. Only in silence can we see and feel the truth. What does it mean to silence our mind? It is to go deep within and find that which is so profound that there are no words to express it. That's what silence is: non-verbal, non-thinking, non-touching, non-seeing, and non-hearing.

When the mind calms, then silence is heard. It's a silence so deep that very few people have ever felt it. This depth of silence is a place where those without courage dare not trespass. Why do they not dare to trespass? Because many people feel that without their five senses there is nothing else to live for. I must say that this is far from the truth. These five senses are created only to bring sense to the world in which we live. Because we see them as physical perceptions that seem concrete and tangible, they give us a false sense of security, a false sense of reality. We are not here to create false perceptions so that our physical selves can feel more powerful or more in control—that defeats our purpose. Rather, we are here to experience the unphysical, the untouchable, the unseeable, and the intangible.

Why is there such an aversion to the intangible aspects of our existence? What are we looking for in life? Are we looking for a comfortable place to lay our body, an assurance that we will be safe, a piece of land that provides security, a role in life that we can control, a paper that verifies our identity, a personality that shows the world who we are? Is this what we think we are here for? To live on this planet and suffer like ghosts without souls?

Open your eyes—even more than that, open your hearts. Let's not succumb to a view that defines us by the limitations of gravity and physicality. The physical world doesn't have the power to reveal our true potential. Its power is to entice us, so that we may enter the world fully absorbed in what it has to offer. It's only then that we see it's just a false show, with great expectations of wholeness, completeness, and happiness. It's the big cosmic trap that sucks us in, only to spit us out when all of our reality is shattered.

So what is left? We may think nothing, but that is not so! At this point, it is time to pull, drag, and force what is left to come forth. We mustn't stop in the middle of the game and give up—that is cowardly. This game must be played until the end to understand the essence of who we truly are.

Shake yourselves, wake yourselves up, there is no more time for sleeping! Your beds are comforting, but your dreams are not. Don't simply be satisfied with what's comfortable, but stop and look at what's uncomfortable. That's where the real journey begins. This discomfort has been avoided over and over throughout your lives. You cannot fool yourselves anymore. Only the truth will shine forth in the end. Have the courage to admit that there is something much deeper within you that you don't know yet. Ask yourself, "What is this unknown part of me that hides like a stranger in my body? Is it my enemy or my friend?"

Then become silent and look for your sixth sense—yes, that intuitive sixth sense that most people don't even know they have. Talk to it. Say, "Wake up sixth sense. Come out, come out, wherever you are. Show your face that has been hidden from me for so long!" This beautiful face has been screaming and crying to be heard, but your fear of knowing your True Self has pushed it even deeper into hiding. This face is calling you, every one of you, to be shown, to be seen. This is your true face, the one you've always had and always will have, the face that doesn't change with age. The one that becomes more and more beautiful every time it looks at itself in the mirror and sees its true reflection. Where is this face to be found? In silence...only in silence.

Let the quietness manifest in every one of your cells and in every thought that arises. Let go of any resistance or insecurity you may have. React to this silent stranger in a warm, loving way, as a parent who has just found his lost child. Awaken this aspect of yourself now. Sit in silence and ask that your innermost Self be revealed.

Don't get discouraged if nothing happens immediately; ask and ask again. Keep on asking, until one day you hear a voice. Don't accept it as your imagination, but realize it is a part of you—a part wanting to get to know you, wanting to unveil your true nature, your true essence.

Take the time to listen very carefully. Let your body take this sixth sense in so that it becomes a comfortable part of you. Pull your Higher Self out of the lost and found...to be found...found forever.

Soul Searching

What is soul searching? It is a popular phrase now, but what is its true meaning? The soul, which is our very essence, has a strong desire to be where it truly belongs—in a place where we have a profound feeling of “coming home.” It's a place that has always existed, where we were born in the beginning, and where we will die in the end. And at the same time, it's a place that has no beginning or end. Many people feel lost and alienated. This is because they have forgotten to look for the soul's home.

So, how do we find our way home? It's not as easy as calling a taxi and asking to be taken home. It's not a place made of four walls, with all of our favorite things inside to keep us comfortable. Nor does it mean that we can travel around the world to find it. Any location in time or space will always be temporary and transient. The home that our soul is searching for has no limits of either time or dimension. It is vast and limitless. It can be found when we have a willingness to seek out every dark corner that exists within ourselves. It is in one of these dark corners that the light may be seen, directing us to the path home.

Why do we feel so far from home? Perhaps because we are afraid of the potential darkness and what may lurk there? What might there possibly be hiding in these dark places—monsters, dragons, leprosy, cancer, demons, enemies, hate, insecurity, fear? We believe that exploring this unknown territory may harm us or even kill us. But once we have the courage to actually look around at these "monsters," we discover that it's only our mind, the greatest trickster of all that's attempting to scare us. Without the fear that the mind produces we would easily be able to explore these monsters (which are only delusions) and discover our own ego at their root. By examining this, we would see that who we really are is not any of these monsters. We would then be able to look deeper and deeper to find the real truth of our existence.

The mind is the negative aspect of a positive soul search. Although soul searching takes us to unknown places, it's the mind that makes it seem so frightening. The mind has put a leash around our necks, taking us on a walk to nowhere. We must stop listening to our mind and begin listening to our soul, if we want to live happier and more authentic lives.

Our soul only wants what's best for us. Its intentions are pure and it will always guide us to make the right choices in life. Our "soul essence" is who we are. We must take the time to listen and ask our soul for advice. There is no reason to ask others for answers that we have within us. It's our *intuition* and not our mind that we can always trust. If we cannot hear our soul speak, then we must listen more carefully until we do. We are not the body, but the soul—which is connected to every other soul. When we truly know this, we will never feel separate and alone again.

Directing Decisions

These two words are easy to understand intellectually for most people, but their meaning seems to disintegrate when it comes to acting them out in everyday life. Life does not play its role by it directing you, but rather by you directing it. When people are unbalanced and live life in a chaotic fashion, they are choosing to let life direct them. But when people decide for themselves what course they will take in life, they are choosing to direct life and to live in harmony with it.

We all have the innate wisdom to know what is best for us at each given moment. We also have the ability to direct and manifest these decisions in our life. Sometimes, however, it seems easier and safer to let others make these choices for us. We do this to protect ourselves from failure and because we then have someone else to blame if we make the wrong decision. But we must become responsible for ourselves. Who wants to live under the wings of another? How devouring and imprisoning this is!

There are many individuals who love to control the lives of others and also many people who want their lives to be controlled; however, these are only “roles” we choose to play in life, because in reality, each and every one of us has the ability to create our own lives.

Life is always changing and that is the beauty of it. For many people, change is very difficult to accept because it often means facing the unknown and this creates a feeling of insecurity. This is so unfortunate because change is actually such a natural and positive force in our lives. It helps make life flow more easily and spontaneously. Change brings with it new thoughts, new ideas, and new ways of doing things. This enables each of us to develop ourselves intellectually, culturally, and spiritually. Stagnation, on the other hand, causes life to degenerate. When we allow others to choose for us and control our lives, we are taking what appears to be the "easy way out." But in reality, giving our power over to another is the more difficult path since it creates much suffering and stagnation in our lives.

You must wake up and realize all the potential that was given to you—befriend it, use it, and love it! You are an individual with your own unique thought process and lifestyle. Who can better tell you what you need than yourself? Who knows you better? Does your mother or father know you better? Does your husband or wife? Does your best friend? Does your priest? I don't think so. You may want to become unconscious and convince yourself that someone knows you better so that you can avoid responsibility, or so that you can blame someone else for the misery in your life. But there is no more time to blame others. There's only time to rise above this behavior and take control of your life. You have always known what's best for you and you always will. Decisions and choices will never cease to exist because they are part of your growing process. Don't stunt your growth and lose the opportunity to make choices freely and innately. Just think how simple and harmonious life would be if you had the ability to make important decisions easily, intuitively, and without confusion and distress. We all have this potential. How can you tap into and use this potential that you have? Let me share with you a few ways:

First, don't allow anyone, no matter who it is, to control you. You are only harming yourself by giving your power over to someone else who could abuse it. No one has the right to take your power from you unless you give it away. So it is up to you to stop this game.

Remember that all the answers to every decision you make in life are inside you. You must first believe this, and then you must listen for the answer. It's so easy to take the advice of others instead of listening to yourself. You may think that they know better, or that they're smarter than you, or that they possibly see more objectively than you. But trusting others, instead of yourself, is a way of putting your life on hold and not taking responsibility for it. Take the time to listen deeply for answers from your intuitive wisdom. If a thought comes through, think about that thought and why it came to you. If you wake up with something on your mind, take the time to ask yourself why. Why was it on your mind and why did you dream about it?

Furthermore, don't expect answers to come easily at the beginning. You must first learn to trust your intuitive voice more and more. It's like learning to ride a bike; it takes time and practice to develop. So have the patience to continue to listen to your intuition, just like you had the patience to learn to ride a bike. The only difference is that one is physical and the other is not.

You must empower and trust yourself to believe that you know what's best for you because there is nobody else who knows you better. Let that "knowing of yourself" be used to inspire and direct your decisions into positive, loving outcomes. You are not here to sabotage yourself. Rather, you are here to enhance every beautiful part of yourself.

So stop listening to another's reality; yours is different, yours is unique, and yours is special. Have not just the respect, but the utmost respect, to honor your life. It's a gift that was given to you that is irreplaceable and indispensable.

Finally, make a promise now. Make a promise that you will direct your life and make decisions that will only enhance and change your life for the better. Realize that it is only you who knows what these decisions are.

Learning to Love Ourselves

What is it that makes us love ourselves? Are we born with self-love or is it something we are taught? Each person comes into this life with a path or a destiny that is followed instinctively, like a driver on automatic pilot. This destiny helps to bring direction and purpose to our lives. It may be a smooth, easy, and loving journey, or it may be a bumpy, hard, and difficult one. Before we are born, our soul chooses which path will serve us best to learn and accomplish what we need. We all have different lessons that are unique for us to learn. We are influenced and driven by the connections we have to people, places, and things. These connections can both help and hinder our capacity for self-love and our progress toward a better life. The love and support we receive from others, such as family, friends, partners, pets, and so forth, help us to connect deeply to each other and creates the strength and confidence we need to achieve our aspirations in the world. Sometimes, however, our relationships can be unhealthy and dysfunctional. This sets us back and even creates phobias, paranoia, sickness, and negative patterns in general. Once we are rooted in this dysfunctional pattern, it's not easy for us to feel and give love generously to ourselves and others. We may not be able to stop these negative circumstances from occurring in our lives, but we can remember them, feel them deeply within our cellular structure, and release them.

The first time a situation occurs, we react spontaneously. But as a similar situation reoccurs, we have the experience to evaluate whether it's healthy or unhealthy. We now have the option to make suitable changes if we see it as being unhealthy. One of the purposes for being in this body is to consciously recognize these unwanted habitual patterns and release them. To some degree, we all have unwanted habits. We carry them with us wherever we go, like overweight baggage that pulls us down. Many of us hope that this load will just disappear by itself. But just like a piece of overweight luggage, it only gets lighter when objects are actually taken out.

So to lighten our load, we must remove negative behaviors from our lives. This often appears so difficult that we pretend these negative behaviors don't exist. But this is only a temporary solution. Periodically, these negative habits will resurface, confronting us again and again, until we finally must face and resolve them. Continually denying these negative patterns causes feelings of depression and unworthiness. As a direct result of this denial, we begin despising ourselves and can even become masochistic. We think that there is no way out of this dilemma and that change is impossible. We then lose all perspective. Feeling hopeless, we become victims to these unwanted patterns. This is not an acceptable way to live.

Our love, the love which is the essence of who we are, must start with *ourselves* and then reach out to others. Like a tree, without its roots to take in food and water and its trunk to firmly define its existence, there would be no growth extending inward or outward. Our trunk (or body), and our roots (or soul), must be nurtured and fed. When a tree is nurtured and loved, it has an abundance of foliage that can offer shade and comfort; when a person is nurtured and loved s/he has abundant health and can then offer love and support to others.

We all have issues in this life that need to be transformed. These issues must not be blindly tolerated and accepted because this kind of attitude will only postpone one's development and growth. Instead, allow these set habits and issues to be recognized. Some might be obvious, like a smoking habit. Others can be more subtle, like deep insecurities. We can begin to identify these negative patterns by first being willing to face them, and then, by using our intuition to see them clearly. After this, we can transform them with mindfulness and awareness into new and healthy patterns that reflect our inner wholeness, love, and perfection.

Demonstrate your love to yourself and see how your trunk and roots will easily grow into stems, leaves, and flowers for you to share with others. Your own blossoming into a whole and loving person is the destiny you should choose for yourself. We all get side tracked sometimes. I'm here to put you back on track—the track you set for yourself.

Capital Punishment

Our brothers and sisters are being murdered every day by our own governments. Capital punishment, which is an act of extreme violence, is not only being tolerated by society, but many times is actually being voted in by the people. Is there no mercy left in this world? Is there only revenge, self-righteousness, and judgment? Have we forgotten to forgive because our hearts are closed and our minds confused? Contrary to common belief, our fears are not eliminated each time a criminal is executed. Even if all criminals were killed, our fears would find someone or something else to blame and destroy. This terrible act of ignorance reveals mankind at its worst. Could it be that we feel if we imitate God, we will be more like God? Even though we cannot giveth, we can surely taketh away. That is a powerful feat, but is it our right to carry it out? It's so easy to judge and condemn another, yet it's so difficult to see what role we, ourselves, play in this barbaric act.

Capital punishment is not really about executing justice; it's about projecting our own unconscious fears onto others. Facing and acknowledging our own fears and inadequacies is so frightening that instead of looking inward where they actually reside, we project both our fears and inadequacies outwards toward others. We spend our whole lives accusing, judging, and blaming others for everything that's wrong in our life. It's the "fault" of our parents, our teachers, our friends, society, and employers, but never ours. Although our life struggles are difficult, this does not give us the right to blame others for our own inadequacies. We must stop deceiving ourselves and pointing our finger at others. Those "others" have nothing to do with us. The criminal is our scapegoat. He provides us with a live drama to watch, judge, and become involved in, making it easier for us to ignore and avoid our own weaknesses and issues.

Our work is to examine all of our fears, recognize them, and release them. If we need to point the finger at someone, we must point it at ourselves. If we need to condemn anything, then we need to condemn all the years we have lived blindly, not seeing the beauty in ourselves and others. If we need to punish someone, then we need to punish ourselves by sacrificing all that belittles us and everyone else. We must respect our soul and everyone else's. No one is any better than anyone else—even a murderer—for I'm sure most of us have had the thought at one time or another of "I wish he was dead," or "I could kill him." Don't be ashamed; be real. Each person who is executed is a human being that had his or her life taken away by other human beings. This is also murder of the first degree. Just because it was voted in and became law does not make it right.

We know that life can be difficult. Anyone who is sensitive and who has been rejected, abandoned, and rarely shown love, can starve to death emotionally. This in turn can cause that person to feel hopeless and desperate and lash out with violence. Where were you when they needed help? More than likely, you were not there. But it is quite likely that you were there when it was time to condemn them to a life behind bars. Where's your love now? Is it also behind bars?

We must open our hearts; we must take the bars away. Only love can put prisons out of business. The caring is the cure, not capital punishment. *All* living creatures are connected to one another. When someone is shot, electrocuted, gassed, or tortured, unconsciously we all feel it, igniting our own feelings of injustice and all the times we have been judged unfairly. We all have felt the injustice of judgment. But instead of taking that injustice and punishing the perpetrator, let's burn the injustice. Let's kill it, and remember it, so we will never hurt another again. Our rational mind, our sincere heart, and our kind soul know far more than our fears know. Besides, fear becomes a hundred times magnified when it is reflected back on itself, collectively.

Take the stand and swear to God that you have come here to live the truth and nothing but the truth. Know that your truth is everyone else's truth—the truth of love, compassion, honesty, and generosity. And if someone has not been fortunate enough to have these qualities in their lives, that you will demonstrate these qualities to them, so that they, too, can benefit and grow into their truth and their purpose.

Dealing with Death

Let death cometh to you like a shadow that covers your body. This darkness represents that which has gone, only to be reborn again with light. Humans seem to dwell on the darkness of the shadow; not knowing that soon after there is an opening of pure white light. What is this shadow that everyone fears so much? This shadow is the part of our existence that has left the physical plane for another realm of existence. Spiritual essence has not been diminished. Nothing has evaporated into thin air. Even the body remains for a while, decomposing slowly to replenish nature.

In our physical reality, the body seems to be of the utmost importance. When the body loses the energy that has kept it alive, earthly reasoning is that everything, including this energy, has ended and no longer exists. This way of thinking has sustained our thought patterns for eons and eons. The idea that everything will die has haunted our lives. We live with this fear of death, believing that one day our lives will suddenly end and we will be thrown into an abyss. How frightening, how shocking this is! Unfortunately, we live our lives with our cells contaminated by this fear of death.

Death is not a means to an end, but rather a passageway that brings us from one side to the other. Like driving inside of a tunnel, there is temporary darkness until we drive out of it and find the light again. The few dark moments we spend inside the tunnel is where our fear begins. We think our life will end here, but this isn't true. Death is a sacred passage and should be treasured rather than feared.

Dualities in life are considered to be opposites. Though opposites represent two points furthest away from each other, taken as a whole they also represent a unit. Years ago, people thought that the earth was flat. Today, we still tend to think in this linear way. This type of thinking is backward and outdated. If we change this idea, understanding that these points are not straight, but rather are circular like the earth is spherical, then we can see that the beginning point and the end point are one. This notion that opposites are completely separate entities has troubled mankind since the beginning of time. When we realize that darkness merges into light, and vice versa, then we understand that all is one. Life and death work exactly the same way. Ultimately, there is no end and no beginning. There is only the merging of life and death, and death and life. The point where life and death meet and merge is a *transformation*.

This transformation could be viewed as a death of sorts, because we have changed our point of view, moving from one realm to another. This transition takes us to a higher level of existence, where truth is seen and oneness is realized. The real gift of life is living with the awareness that death is to be cherished. Death is the bringing together of light and darkness, making our life whole and complete. Death is the part of life that binds the circle together and completes it, so a new circle may begin to form, which is more evolved and wiser.

Death is actually pure white light. It is a natural process that all life forms experience, from a rock, to a flower, to an insect, to a bird, to an animal, to a human being. No one is spared the experience of death. It is our last sacred rite where we can give thanks for the gift of life.

We must let death into our hearts and our souls. We must treat it as if it were our very best friend, and know that when the time comes, our best friend will be there to walk us to the other side.

Death is a natural process that raises us from one consciousness to another. It must be respected and loved instead of denied and feared. The result of our denial of death has been pain, depression, despair, and separation—from ourselves and our Creator. Enough! We must now see death as a teacher who wants to reveal the most cherished secrets of existence to us. When the moment of death arrives, we will now welcome it and be ready for a new journey.

You may ask, "How can I make death a part of my life now, so I may be prepared when the time comes?" Here are some suggestions:

It is so important to live life in the here and now, so stop living your life in the fear that you will die one day. This is living one quarter of the potential you were meant to live. The fear of death stops us from doing the things we really want to do. It holds us back, only to make us feel regretful in later years that we didn't live our lives fully.

Recognize and declare that one day you, too, will pass to the other side of the tunnel. No one is exempt from this, no matter how many fountains of youth are discovered. Look at death as if it were a subject in school that you are studying. Read books about death to become familiar with the subject. Tibetan Buddhism has many exercises dealing with death. Authors such as Stephen Levine, Elizabeth Kübler-Ross, and others write beautifully on the subject.

The fear of death has created many illnesses born out of non-acceptance. Accept your death as you accept your life. Know that it is something beautiful to prepare yourself for, like a birthday or a wedding day. Don't wait until it's too late. Ask death to reveal its innermost secrets to you. It is willing and waiting.

Talk about death instead of hiding and denying its existence. Listen to other people's views. There are those who have died and returned, only to tell their loving stories about death. Many people have also had personal contact with deceased loved ones, proving to them that there is life after death.

Remember that death is not the end of existence; rather, it is a passageway to a higher state of being. It is a transformation. Although the unknown is frightening, consider all of those life events you have had the courage to face without knowing the consequences, and realize that this same courage can be accessed to face and accept death.

Know that life is a teaching, and one important aspect of this teaching is to trust in your life's purpose—that your life was meant for something very meaningful and you are here to find that meaning. Don't stop at the first stop sign you find, but search deeper for your true purpose. Take the time to enter a higher realm that always shows there is reason for your existence. Try to connect through meditation, contemplation, or prayer to your higher self—it is patiently waiting to be contacted. It's there, where all the truths are found, inside you and only you, your true God-Self. Be thankful that you have the opportunity to be able to search this subject out. I'm sure that there are many souls who have wished they had, but for them it's too late.

May life be with you, and may death be with you. Only then will you realize that they are both one and the same.

Creating Creativity

There is nothing so natural as creativity. It's in our flesh and bones; it's in our blood and cells. Every part of us physically, emotionally, mentally, or spiritually can access our creativity at any given moment. We were born to create that which flows from our essence and then outwardly manifest it here on earth.

Each person's creative energy is as individual as each person's face. There are various facets of this energy in our cells, and when they are put together as a whole, they define our special and unique creativity. If one facet is stronger than the others, then that one will dominate the others and be used more in everyday life. The dominating facet, however, is still only a tiny fragment of our creative force. Most people stop at this small amount of creativity and go no further. They are satisfied with this miniscule amount because it can be tapped into easily without effort.

There would be no limit to our creativity if we were to utilize most or all of it. Because of our fear of possibly failing, the limitations we place on ourselves are tremendous. Most of the time, this fear is an illusion created by our mind to distract us from the accomplishments we were meant to achieve in this life. But the only way to counter this ploy of the mind, and accomplish what we were meant to, is by opening ourselves up to the vulnerability of failure. Yet the majority of people stop a creative project at the first sign of failure and never continue. This is considered an act of cowardliness in the eyes of the great masters. Today, most people convince themselves that they are just "playing it safe" by stopping a creative project.

Their reasoning goes something like this: "If I play it safe, I will not be seen as a fool. I haven't lost anything monetarily, and I really haven't failed because I stopped before I finished the project." However, thinking like this is an excuse that automatically limits our great potential. The urge to create is constantly coming up during our life span. Each time we ignore it, we push our creativity down deeper and deeper, making it more and more difficult to be realized.

Creative power is the most potent energy on earth. In fact, there wouldn't even be an earth if it hadn't once been created. There wouldn't be a you, or a me, or any other living thing in this world without the act of creation. Why is it, then, that the most beautiful attribute that exists within us—our creativity—has been minimized and limited?

Our relationship to nature is similar to our relationship with creativity. We minimize nature; therefore, we do not honor it as the creator and nurturer of life. Nature is our greatest teacher, showing us how to live in peace and harmony and how to emulate its rhythms and strength. Why is it that we are limiting and destroying that which gives us life? Must humans first destroy everything positive before they can realize and appreciate its value? How could this happen? How can this still be happening?

Without the creative force circling freely throughout our bodies, we feel unsatisfied, frustrated, lazy, and unmotivated. Unfortunately, these are the feelings that dominate many of us, the feelings that we wake up to every morning. No wonder there is so much despair and hopelessness felt in the world. What could give you more hope than for me to say to you that everyone—*and I mean everyone*—has the full potential to wake up their innate creative power and manifest it in a life that is full and satisfying.

We are denying our own potential when we compare ourselves to others and acknowledge their gifts without acknowledging our own gifts. For example, when we say, "Oh well, she's so talented, so smart, no wonder she's so successful and I'm not," this statement shows our lack of belief in ourselves. In truth, everyone has the same unlimited potential. The question is, are we willing to seek it out? Are we willing to risk failure to become a success?

Tell me, what are your limits to finding this creativity which is already inside of you? Ask yourself, "What are the obstacles to discovering my source of creativity? What are my fears? How can I let these fears go? What are my interests? What comes easy to me? What have I always wanted to do or be in my life but was afraid to try? What types of things fill my body and soul with joy?" The answers to these questions are all signs of our creative juices at work. They are the very passions that our soul craves to develop.

Success is not based on how much money we can make from our passion. Success happens by opening ourselves up to our creative potential and allowing our true nature to unfold. If we do this, our true expression of who we really are will manifest, bringing with it a sense of wholeness and completeness. Isn't that why we are here? Aren't we here to truly express who we really are and to transform this world into a better, more loving, and creative place for everyone?

In our world with its many problems, you may say, "This sounds so idealistic. A transformation of this magnitude could never occur through such a simple act." Then don't pursue your creativity for others or for the world; instead, do it for yourself. After all, it's you that has to live with yourself. So start now on the courageous quest for your true creative potential. I assure you that this will inspire others to do the same. Be one of the first to fully manifest your creativity. It's your duty; it's your life.

Family Ties

We needn't look any further than our own family to heal ourselves and our world. Without healing ourselves first, in reality, it is impossible to heal others. When we have not investigated our own issues, or our shadow side, we project them unconsciously onto others. This projection gets in the way of seeing ourselves and others clearly and creates disharmony in our lives and in our world.

Family must be treated as a world within itself. For many years, it was our only world. When there is truth and sincerity in the nuclear family, then that is what's projected out into the larger world and positive changes can occur. Because of this, it is important that we devote time and energy with our own families. Yet, this is what many people resist and where they stop, because working with one's own family is difficult and often extremely painful. Our relationship to our family must be looked at seriously. We must learn new ways to communicate more honestly with our family members.

The nature of life is to grow and evolve. If we live in the past and continue to relate to our families in dysfunctional ways, this just perpetuates the suffering and the miscommunication that is already rampant in society. We must not fear that by altering these old patterns we will hurt ourselves or family members. This is not so! In most cases, by getting rid of family patterns which no longer serve us (be it denial, dependency, co-dependency, victimizing, controlling, etc.), we can break open new paths. Here we can create healthy relationships based on love, respect, and truth.

This is not to say that every aspect of our family relationships needs overhauling. It's only those parts that have rusted and decayed with time that need our close attention. All living organisms in the universe experience transformation. This is a natural process, like a caterpillar turning into a butterfly. These transformations are also a natural part of our human process. However, if we are afraid of this change, we will stunt our growth and remain like children our entire lives. The basis for true transformation is our capacity to be open and honest.

Every person brings his or her life-challenges into their relationships. When problems arise a change of partners can become an option. As time goes on, one realizes that with each new partner comes a new set of problems or the same old ones. It is helpful to examine the things that we are carrying into each of our relationships. Old baggage that we bring with us hasn't worked for us in the past, doesn't work for us now, and most likely will not work for us in the future. Where do these patterns stem from? Most often from childhood and our relationship to family—that's why I keep emphasizing the need to heal family relationships first! By doing this, the meaning and the truth of what we learn will seep into other parts of our life. For example, if we are hiding feelings from our family, we are surely hiding feelings from other significant relationships in our life as well; they go hand in hand.

In the final analysis, it all comes down to the question: "Are you being honest with yourself?" For many who habitually hide their feelings from others, this is a very difficult question to answer. It worries me that so many can no longer recognize the trait of true honesty. Can you? It's important to present your True Self to the world, be it beautiful or ugly, for we are all equal and each one of us has both aspects. Accept your weaknesses as you accept your strengths. Once you have accomplished that, you will be able to accept those traits in your family and others.

A key aspect in the healing of self and family is to stop making judgments—beginning first with judgments about yourself. Do not look within yourself and label certain aspects as good and others as bad. It is unkind and unwise of you to judge some of your "true" feelings as acceptable and others unacceptable. With judgment comes shame, blame, and guilt, resulting in hiding your true self. Let go of judging and you will free yourself and others from recreating these lessons lifetime after lifetime! Ask yourself, "What do I have to hide?" Is it more important than *truth*?

Vow this very day to fully commit to truth, knowing that you do this not only to heal yourself, but also to heal your family, your friends, and the world. As you work on healing yourself, you will be able to see more clearly the harm that has been done to the world by those who have expressed less than the truth. As you come to realize the impact of your commitment, you will desire to work even harder on truthfulness, openness, and honesty. *Nothing* is more important than truth. It is what existence is created from…it is what calls out to you. Do not close your ears; let your essence feel its rapture. Let it feed your soul and then let it speak the whole truth, and nothing but the truth, so help you God.

Our Higher Self

Who is it we want to get to know?
Our higher self.
Who is it that is a stranger to us?
Our higher self.
Who is it that we deeply know more than anyone else?
Our higher self.

Who is it we forget to listen to?
Our higher self.
Who is it that connects us to God?
Our higher self.
Who is it that knows all truth?
Our higher self.

Who is it we are constantly doubting?
Our higher self.
Who is it that shows us the shining light?
Our higher self.
Who is it that teaches us our lessons?
Our higher self.

Who is it that tells us we are making a mistake?
Our higher self.
Who is it that patiently waits for our perfection?
Our higher self.
Who is our best friend?
Our higher self.

Who is it that's pushing us to take a risk?
Our higher self.
Who is it that's open to new ideas?

Our higher self.
Who is it that lives in the moment?
Our higher self.

Who is it that has no concept of time?
Our higher self.
Who is it that wants to be free?
Our higher self.
Who is it that gives clarity to our mind?
Our higher self.

Who is it that remains when our body dies?
Our higher self.
Who is it that pushes us on the road to spirituality?
Our higher self.
Who is it that loves us unconditionally?
Our higher self.

Who is it that knows all answers?
Our higher self.
Who is it we need to ask the next time we are confused?
Our higher self.
Who helps us live a more harmonious and peaceful life?
Our higher self.

Who is it we need to get closer to?
Our higher self.
Who is it, this thing called our higher self?
A sage, a guru, an enlightened being?
No need to go searching for it.
Just welcome it and invite it in.

Metamorphosis

Like a caterpillar that is physically transformed into a butterfly, our bodies are constantly moving and changing both physically and mentally. They are like waves breaking on the shore; no one wave is ever the same. Each is always creating anew its own style and form. Our bodies are also continually transforming in this ocean of life. Will we learn how to swim in order to facilitate our relationship with the ocean? Or will we fear the water, dipping only our feet in?

Transmutation is our natural way of expressing our development and evolution. However, many of us choose to stay like a caterpillar forever, crawling from one path to the next, too afraid to trust the natural process of life. On the other hand, the caterpillar doesn't fear that its form will change into a butterfly; rather, it naturally accepts this ever evolving process.

The metamorphosis from a caterpillar to a butterfly drastically changes its view and allows the caterpillar to gain a broader perspective on life. When a caterpillar turns into a butterfly, it is no longer constricted to just dirt, grass, rocks, trees, and crawling slowly from one leaf to the next. Instead, the caterpillar ends up flying and seeing further than it ever could have imagined. As the caterpillar's outer horizons greatly expand, its inner horizons expand, too. The qualities the caterpillar received as it crawled, like patience, persistency, and sensibility, are deeply grounded by its connection to the earth and this helps it to prepare for becoming a butterfly. Once it becomes a butterfly, each of these qualities helps it in countless ways.

Like the caterpillar's metamorphosis into a butterfly, we change from infancy to childhood, then to adulthood, and finally to old age. The difference, though, is the caterpillar makes this change without resistance or hesitation. The change is a natural process the caterpillar innately accepts without fear. This graceful acceptance of "what is" allows its life to unfold effortlessly. You may say, "But caterpillars have no choice since nature dictates what comes next." This is so, but doesn't nature also dictate what comes next for humans? If we would only listen to nature. But the problem is, humans don’t listen because we have highly developed minds that we rely on to make most of our decisions in life. That’s the main difference between a caterpillar/butterfly and a human being.

Although the mind is useful in many ways, it is not our only source of intelligence. Like the butterfly, we have a natural God-given "intuitive wisdom" that follows the dictates of nature. This wisdom is always accessible to us if we trust it and tune into its quiet voice. Its concern is always for our highest good and it wants to guide us to our greatest potential.

We must learn to decipher when to use our mind and when to use our intuitive wisdom. Attaining a fine balance between the use of our mind-intelligence and our intuitive-intelligence is our task in life. Because the natural state of the mind is to fear and doubt, it can't be trusted to make life-changing decisions. Because the mind is concerned with comfort and security, it is afraid of the unpredictable and the unknown. Furthermore, it is not concerned with living in the moment; rather, it dwells on the past and the future. Because we follow our minds' dictates instead of our hearts' dictates, our transmutations have diminished into stagnancy and decay.

This has eroded our lives and chipped away much of our life force. When we follow nature's way and listen to our intuitive wisdom, we accept what arises. This results in our living in the present where transformation is welcomed and natural. By living our lives like this, we live in a serene state of being and may be seen by some as enlightened souls. In truth, enlightenment is the natural state for all of us.

Our sister the caterpillar/butterfly is our mentor to follow and imitate. She is our teacher, for we can see how gracefully she flows with life. As a butterfly, she moves on to higher planes. And so would we, if only we listened to our heart instead of our head.

A butterfly's life is probably the most perfect life we could ask for. Think about it: the butterfly is free to explore and move where it desires; it eats free and healthy food from one flower to the next; it is beautiful and graceful; it lives each moment to its fullest; it can fly with ease; and it loves its life without questioning it. We would benefit tremendously if we chose to live life in much the same way as the butterfly. In certain ways, our life *is* similar to the caterpillar/butterfly. We begin life as a baby, crawling like a caterpillar and innocently exploring every object we can touch. As we grow and begin walking upright, our horizons expand and our experiences multiply. This is the point where most people choose to remain a caterpillar instead of choosing to become a butterfly. Our cocoon has the capacity to become our hell or our heaven. We can choose to live in our cocoon, afraid of life's opportunities and challenges, or we can choose to emerge loving and open to every moment that life gives us.

Our choice is not already written in the stars; our choice is not imprinted in our destiny. Rather, it is unknown, like the day we will die. Instead of fearing transformation, we must embrace it and move forward like a butterfly. If we embrace it, we will evolve into a beautiful, spontaneous, totally aware and conscious human being.

This is our natural way. Let's respect our mentors—the plants, the insects, and animal kingdom—and follow their path. They are here to remind us to return to the right track if we stray. Let's create our own destiny and choose to commit to nature's way. This is the true way…the intuitive way…our way.

Embracing Infinite Energy

People always seem to ask, when did the beginning begin? I am here to tell you that there is no beginning and there is no end. There are only beginnings when there are ends. What we have here is not a beginning or an end, but a consistency of energy that is continuously flowing. This energy is always with us; it can be felt at any time. It is the basis of who we truly are. We vibrate like a machine plugged into an electrical socket. Our energy is more subtle, however, and less noticeable than electricity. This is why it seems to us more difficult to tune into it. Because our energy cannot be accessed from an outside source, like electricity from a socket, we must generate it ourselves. This is something we must learn again, since we have lost our innate feeling of it.

Our energy is constantly moving, like our heart beats. It's a great pounding of vibrational energy, dancing around the ethereal body. It cannot usually be seen, but is always felt and is the basis of life, movement, and change. When we are in tune with our energy, we are fully balanced, our life unfolds spontaneously, and we intuitively know what our next step is. The result of not being attuned to our energy is chaos and fear.

Our energy does not need to be controlled since it knows how to move naturally. It is so natural that we don't have to do anything, or go anywhere, to find it. It is what we are made of and without it we would not exist. We must let it flow within us naturally, and not try to catch it as if we were trying to catch an animal to place in bondage. How can energy be caught when it is always here? We must recognize its existence and realize that many times the things that are *unseen* are more important than the things that are seen. We need to alter our priorities and recognize that the physical world is only a stepping stone to the unseen spiritual world. We must learn to feel this energy and strengthen it, so that it can flow freely through the body. To learn to do this is of the utmost importance.

You may ask, "How can I feel this energy flowing through my body?" You must first see yourself as light. Visualize a glow of light that surrounds your body. See this light and start to breathe in and out. The light moves in your body when you inhale, and moves out of your body when you exhale. This light is like waves in the ocean, constantly moving in and out. Let this light become your body, so that you no longer have a body, only light vibrating in and out. Then affirm that this is who you really are, and that this pure light within you is always connected to the true Source of all light and color.

Color is also vibrational, just like you are, and joins your energy to help balance, heal, and transform you, so that you may become whole again.

If you were to ask, "What do I look like vibrationally?" the closest answer would be a rainbow. That's why we love them so much. Rainbows reflect our wholeness. When negative emotions such as fear or anger arise in us, color fades from our body, creating imbalance and causing illness. Each color represents a facet of us. When a color is missing, a part of us is missing, too. The color must be brought back in, to enliven our vibration and to heal ourselves. When we are whole and healthy our energy is bright and full of every color.

When you are out of balance, it is important to ask yourself, "What color do I need to make myself whole again?" If you are quiet and centered, you will receive an answer. Usually, the color you need is the first color that comes to mind. You can then visualize putting this color into your body and letting every cell absorb it.

Be aware of this light that you are, and you will be shown the right path. And what is the right path? One that offers never ending choices and challenges. This is a path of love and light—it is without beginning or end—it is infinite and it leads you back to your True Self.

Reclaiming Your Birthright

Reclaim your birthright. You are a child of God and you have the same rights as God. However, from birth you have been told that you are separate and less than God. So, you go on believing this all of your life until one day your body dies and your soul realizes that this is not the case. Is it your fault that you believed your elders, the ones who were supposed to know so much more?

Our lives are constantly being challenged by new ideas and new revelations. It is we who must decide which of these feel true and which feel false. The problem, however, is that we have been accepting our parents' views for too long. To conform to the views of our parents or those of society without questioning them first is taking the easy way out. It is always our choice to continue, or not to continue, in the footsteps of our ancestors. We must look deeply to see if their beliefs really "ring true" for us. Many of us believe that thinking differently from our parents would be disrespectful. Others just never question the established view. To reclaim our birthright, we must realize that we have a choice in everything we think or do. We mustn't any longer just automatically accept the mainstream view of others because it can be deceiving.

Why have you been born into this precious life? Have you ever asked this question? If you start to think about it, you would realize that it is probably the most pertinent question that you could ever ask. If you haven't asked this question before, why not? Is it because you don't really care? Is it possible that you're afraid to investigate this question? Or could it be that you think no one really knows the answer to this important question?

As a child you may have gone to Sunday, Bible, Hebrew, or any other religious school. If so, did these schools make you feel good? Did they answer your inquisitive questions about life? Think about it, for maybe it was at this time that you turned off your innate desire to know about God and began to settle for less. You may have gone home after a disturbing talk at Sunday school and asked your parents, "Why would God allow someone to be punished if God is so loving?" And perhaps no one could answer this question properly for you. If this felt hypocritical to you, you may have done the most natural thing that came to you—turned away from religion, thinking it better to believe in no God than a God who judges and hurts people. And in separating yourself from God you may have put more value on external things, believing that at least material things give some satisfaction and they don't judge anyone.

If you believed in your family's religion, you might have embraced such beliefs without questioning them because you desired to be accepted by your family, peers, or society. Tell me then, how deep is your commitment to spirituality? And how fulfilled and connected are you to God? I'll tell you that many of you have lost your spirituality and that you have become a society of half believers. As a substitute for true spirituality, some of you have immersed yourselves in addictions and indulgences to numb the pain. Why do you feel so much pain? It is because you feel separated and alienated from your Creator and your Self. It is because you have chosen to accept no God than a judgmental God who inflicts guilt and injustices. And it is because you cannot go along with a God that commits acts that are in opposition to what you feel is innately right that the belief there is no God is born. What can I say, except that I understand and sympathize with you. It is better to believe in no God than a God who goes against all of your intuitive knowing.

Understanding this, we must begin to look beyond the limited ideas that have been accepted by society. We must see the bigger picture, like a photo that's been enlarged to notice every tiny detail. Our religions are not working. They divide us more than they unite us. Many wars are started from religious-based ideas. What does that tell us? It tells us that we are not being told the whole truth.

I, as many other saints, fought during my lifetime for the right to express my true beliefs about God. The Church resented this, but I continued to fight for self-expression and the beliefs that God revealed to me. In those days, people conformed to traditional religious teachings without questioning them. My followers believed in me, for they felt my utter devotion to Jesus and God. Each and every disciple was allowed to have their own experience of what God meant to them. I did not deny them their individual relationship with God, but sacredly *honored* it.

Our religions, nowadays, do not abide by this. They expect and demand that everyone feel the same towards God and that certain rules and regulations be obeyed or one is damned to hell. Many religions arbitrarily judge our acts believing some of these acts warrant going to hell and others warrant going to heaven. Who but God can really determine this? Wars are started and our own brothers and sisters are killed over someone's interpretation of right and wrong. I say that this is rubbish—there is no clear line that distinguishes hell from heaven. Where does God lie, on the side of heaven? Who created hell and the devil? Is the devil more powerful than God, and is that why there is so much injustice, sickness, and war? Should we be worshipping Satan instead of God? Or did God the Almighty Power create the devil, and if so, why? Or maybe God is also the devil embracing all that exists on this planet. Maybe God created the devil so we as humans could decide which side we choose to be on. It may be possible that God and the devil are best friends working together to see who will win. As the world turns today, who knows who will win? It looks like Satan is ahead of the game. Is God losing His grip? Is evil stronger than love? If God created Satan, why is Satan so powerful? Is this God's choice or our choice? Are we turning away from God because we believe more in what the devil represents, or could it be that God and the devil are one and the same? Why not love Satan as much as we love God, or better yet, why not see God and Satan as one, the two together expressing all human behavior?

All of us have our God-like side as well as our shadow side. Our dark side, which is made up largely of our fears, does play a very important role in our existence. Pushing our fears away like they were strangers will only stop us from getting to know them. Let's befriend and accept our fears so that we can love them, for they are part of us. By accepting and understanding them, our fears no longer have such a negative power over us. Like a grandmother or grandfather who has passed to the other side, we must cherish them and then release them.

Because we live in a dualistic world, Satan will always be a part of it. He is the other side of God. It's for us to decide and choose what is true for us. God does not decide for us nor does He judge us. We are His children, connected by our Souls. Our individual soul chooses our own path and how we want to live it. We must not blame God or Satan, but instead take responsibility ourselves for the choices we have made that determine how our life is unfolding. We must not judge Satan because he is not a demon, but only a device used so we may see both sides of the coin. Neither side is wrong, only one is contrary to the other. If there were just one side, there would be no choice. Instead, God has made a world of infinite possibilities, so that we may determine for ourselves what feels true to us.

Don't follow in your parents' or society's footsteps, but instead make your own imprint in the sand. Your individual and unique footprint is your gift from God. Use it and love it, for it is your own identity that walks with you. Make a full imprint; press deep into the sand to find its truth. Your "feet" are what ground and stabilize you. Let them feel the earth and also touch the stars, for you are of the two realms. Respect and feel wholeness from this. *You are one with God*! God wants you to apprehend this.

It is God's wish that each and every one of you profoundly touch the part of your Self that is connected to God, for only then will you be able to embrace life. God asks you to reclaim your birthright and join in an all out celebration and recognition that you have all the truths within you. You are God's *expression*, so express yourself deeply, passionately and compassionately, without guilt, without shame, and without judgment. Accept your Self. God does and always will.

Seeing Problems as Blessings

What is a problem? In essence, there are *no* problems. Problems stem from the perception we have that something is not working. We think it is not working because we are either not meeting it head on, combating it, or believe it accidentally came from outside ourselves.

In actuality, it's these so called "problems," or the things in our life that seemingly aren't working, that actually help us to make better decisions and choose our actions more carefully. Actions always create reactions. Many times we have no idea how a reaction will unfold. Should this uncertainty stop us from taking the action? At times it does. It stops us from flowing with "what is" because we are afraid of what the outcome from the action might be. We struggle with making choices and decisions and often avoid taking any action, hoping we can live a life free of consequences.

It is because we resist our problems that they seem so difficult. This resistance often causes us to feel depressed, overwhelmed, and out of control. We believe that these problems have no reason for existing other than to make our lives miserable. So we continue to view them as enemies who are only here to harm us. It is this way of thinking about problems that actually causes our misery, not the problems themselves. Our mind is creating what we feed it—it is as simple as that. When we choose to avoid problems, more problems arise. Often they arise before the original ones are resolved. So we end up with a line of problems outside our door, knocking loudly to come in. That's when we get angry and lock the door, screaming "Enough!" Frequently, nothing is dealt with at that point and our lives become more and more complicated.

If we could learn to recognize that life's problems actually contribute to an understanding of who we are, we would view them differently instead of resisting and avoiding them. We would see that our problems act as mirrors…mirrors that show us where our energy is blocked and needs to open. Life's problems really are our guides and mentors, showing us which direction we need to take and what we need to move towards. In truth, our problems are our helpers, enabling us to see that the obstacles we face are there for a purpose.

Problems are really blessings in disguise. We should give thanks for their existence rather than fearing them, avoiding them, and despising them. They reveal to us what our soul is craving to work on—to what it wants to complete. Our essence brings us these problems so that we may confront them and then work through them. How lucky we are! Each issue that needs to be worked on is automatically brought forth by our essence. We don't even have to think about what area of concern to bring up next—it's all done for us.

Rather than avoiding a problem or creating a huge story around it, we should invite it in, work with it, resolve it, and then let it go. When we understand *why* we have a problem, it becomes easier to accept and to work with. The solution then becomes more obvious. The obstacle dissolves, allowing the next "problem" the room it needs to be resolved.

Accepting problems, instead of resisting them, brings an inner sense of lightness and relaxation. This opens us so that we can resolve problems using our intuitive wisdom. Using our intuitive wisdom with our creative energy to solve a problem is one of the most satisfying feelings there is. The problem's resolution is our reward for addressing it instead of avoiding it.

Life works in a magnificent way. It presents itself to us symbolically as a path of stones, each stone appearing just when we are ready to step on it, one stone in front of the other. Each stone represents a problem, and the stones together make up the path, and the path leads to freedom. This freedom brings us home—home to where we started, home to where problems are nonexistent, home to where only peace prevails. That is what we are all working towards, and where, sooner or later, we'll all end up: *It's for you to choose when.*

Here are some guidelines for Problem Solving:

- See the problem as a challenge rather than an obstacle.
- Know that your Higher Self brought the problem into your life so that you can work through it to find resolution.
- Ask the problem why it came to you and what purpose it has in your life.
- Surrender to the problem, letting it be your teacher and thus opening yourself to a solution.
- Use the problem as a learning experience to avoid making the same mistakes over and over again.

Possessions

How many things do you have in your possession? Do these things make your life fulfilled and happy? It may seem so, for these possessions do give us a feeling of elation and gratification when they are first acquired. These feelings enable us to momentarily forget our pending problems. But our forgetfulness is short lived. It isn't long before our problems resurface, capturing our attention and causing us to forget about our new possessions. It's not that possessions are intrinsically bad; rather, it's that the motive behind their purchase needs to be examined. The motive is usually overlooked, however, and we never examine why we do the things we do. Many times in a single day, we act unconsciously, following our impulses and believing that they are our true desires. And we never investigate them any further.

How many of us actually believe that we are here on earth mainly to obtain possessions? Is this our purpose—to work our whole life—so that we can make enough money to buy what our heart desires? We seem to think that this is what our heart really wants, but maybe this is only what we've been taught to believe. If we investigate further, we find that once a possession is acquired, buying another one is already on our minds. It never ends—the more we have, the more we want. It becomes an addiction. We begin to believe that we must have these things to survive. We think that possessing things will relieve the emptiness we feel inside. This might work temporarily, but before long the feeling of emptiness returns and we are then busily looking for the next thing to possess.

Tell me, how many of you are addicted to consuming things? And why do you feel that these things will bring you fulfillment? Maybe it is because deep inside you are longing to feel whole. Maybe it is because you're feeling that you are missing a big piece of who you really are. We *have* lost touch with the true meaning of why we are here. We've limited our development to accepting whatever the mind tells us. Unfortunately, our mind doesn't know who we really are and what we really need. A part of us has been greatly influenced by an external world that believes we need to consume many items in order to be fulfilled. This part of us then rationalizes every reason why we should have them.

Now as I said before, possessions are not bad in and of themselves because they do make life more comfortable and enjoyable. The important thing is that we fully understand this is their only function. If we place an unrealistic value on them, hoping that with the next thing we acquire our emptiness will disappear, we forget their true purpose. Remember: *no-thing* can ever fill the void.

We must stop this vicious cycle of continually acquiring things *now*. It is not working. Instead, it is hindering us mentally and financially. Consumerism helps the economy, but not our soul. Our soul has no interest in physical objects. Its only desire is that our God-like qualities be awakened so that love and peace will prevail within each and every one of us. Our soul knows what we truly need to possess. Often we don't listen to it because we are so used to listening to the mind. This causes our soul to feel like a stranger in our lives. The soul wants us to know it just as we know the body and the mind.

But it can't force us, for only we can choose what's important in our life.

Some people are realizing that their possessions tie them down and are more of a burden than a joy. These are the lucky few who have mostly been raised with physical comforts in their life. Often we must first have the comforts of life in order to be able to give them up later. Through the experience of having them and then later choosing to give them up, we learn that possessions don't equal happiness. This experience also teaches that we must learn to search deeper within ourselves to find something more meaningful. It's time for everyone to look beyond the physical and start to possess that which is unphysical. It really is quite easy. We don't have to stop possessing . . . it's just that what we decide to possess must change.

Wouldn't we be happier possessing love rather than a TV? Or peace of mind instead of a Mercedes? Or joy rather than a computer? Or harmony instead of a stereo? If not, then we need to investigate what our priorities are. People rarely work on obtaining the intangible *inner* possessions. This is not because they are unwanted; rather, it's because they are more difficult to attain.

Working on building our inner qualities is much more valuable and rewarding than any items we could possibly buy in the external world. For example, the great love that we feel for someone special could never compare to a physical possession we own. Love not only feels wonderful, it's also free. Unfortunately, we tend to believe that if something is free, it has no worth.

It's how much love we have in our life that determines our real happiness, not how many cars we have in the garage.

So let's explore our inner possessions more, since they reflect our true identity. When we do develop our inner attributes, we find that we enjoy our physical possessions even more. This is because we are no longer obsessed with them or trapped by their hold on us. We discover that we are just as happy without them as we are with them. We see that by giving up our desire for things, we are freed to use our energy in more beneficial ways. Generally, much of our lives revolve around fulfilling our desires. This uses up at least eighty percent of our energy. So we work to have and we have to work. We do this to be able to earn enough money to buy all the latest things on the market that we want. This is all consuming.

Let's begin to give up this endless cycle. We can then use our energy to build our lives on a strong foundation of the profound truths we already possess. We must wake up from our deep sleep and realize that this incredible life we are each given is a gift from God—completely free of charge. Let's find the precious possessions that exist within us, for they are actually what we have come here to experience. Love, joy, truth, peace, and harmony are our birthright and our paths to salvation.

We need to take the time to be silent and examine our life. We must think and decide for ourselves what is important to us in life, what our true priorities are. We mustn't stop at the first impulse and accept it, since it is probably too shallow to be the truth. Instead, we must dive deeper to where the more profound answers are. We must lie beside these answers and embrace them, for to know them is to know the real you. It takes determination and courage to delve deep into the unknown and find all the answers that are hiding behind dark corners. But I ask you, why keep these answers dormant and asleep? Why keep yourself unconscious and irresponsible when you have the potential to discover what the answers are that will transform your life?

Go inside. Go where every delicious possession of yourself is waiting to be tasted so that it can be digested, assimilated, and known. May you know the true you, *for no one else will* if you don't.

The Destructive Flames of Blame

It's not easy to forgive, especially if someone has harmed us physically, mentally, or emotionally. The sense of violation we feel causes us to build walls around ourselves to shield us from future hurts. We protect ourselves so well that even the feelings of love and joy are blocked from our body, mind, heart, and soul. We become numbed and hardened from the past experiences we've had. These experiences, however, are not meant to close us off from life; rather, they are created for us to "re-examine" our intentions and choices.

These seemingly arbitrary experiences that can be so hurtful do have a purpose in our lives. Like a soap opera, our minds create drama. Drama allows us to feel life's events profoundly. Even though it may cause us great sorrow, drama helps us to see what works, or what doesn't work, in our lives. Blaming ourselves or others for unwanted circumstances in life will not help us to resolve these difficult situations. Instead, it prolongs and complicates them further. Blaming often fuels the situation with hate and revenge. This entangles us even deeper, causing us pain and wasting our energy. If we accept that all life's situations have a purpose and that they manifest for our highest good, who can we blame?

Blaming others keeps us locked in the past. Only when we are able to forgive ourselves and others will we be set free to live in the present. Living in the past keeps us from developing. We find ourselves attracting the same energy over and over, re-creating similar events in our lives. This pattern continues, until one day, we are finally able to see clearly what we've been doing. An actual *shift* in our perception occurs.

This shift allows us to better understand our negative patterns and to gain a new outlook on ourselves. This new perception enables us to expand and create a more beneficial life.

Many times, however, we get frustrated with ourselves for not understanding these patterns faster. We may think, "What's wrong with me? Why do I make the same mistakes over and over?" There is no need to be so critical with yourself, for you are doing the best you can. It's your intuitive wisdom acting through your will that eventually initiates change. Repeatedly re-enacting the same issue slowly builds your courage to face it and transcend it. Your intuition always has the patience to wait until the pattern is played out completely and no longer is needed in your life.

Holding on to the role of victim and blaming others only keeps the issue burning out of control like a wild fire. This fire must be put out or it will scorch your very existence. Forgive yourself for all of your perceived inadequacies and know that they serve a purpose. Forgive yourself for taking so long "to get it right" and know that there is a reason for this. Forgive yourself, in general, and forgive others, too. Without others, you could not act out your part, giving you the experience to transform that which is not working in your life. Your experience is your script in life, your performance is your role in life, and your practice is what gives you the courage to move on to your next scene, which hopefully is wiser and more evolved.

The Pollution of Regret

Life is a spontaneous movement. Like a teeter-totter, it moves up and down. When regret is felt, this swinging stops, delaying and hindering life's next move. To feel regret is to put a hold on life and to stop its natural movement.

Does regret inspire us to change our ways? The fact is, be it right or wrong, there is no turning back when an action is taken. Time does not repeat itself; it only lives for the second and then moves on to the next second. Regret, however, lives in the past, wishing that the past would reappear so that the action could be changed. Remorse, then, infiltrates the mind and body, polluting both, and causing us to believe in the "shoulds" and "coulds" of life. When we live in the "shoulds and coulds" of life, we are living in the past, where regret resides. When we live in truth, we are living in the present moment, where love and peace reside.

We all express ourselves by the actions we demonstrate throughout our life. Each action taken is either spontaneous or planned. Does it make a difference if an action which you considered to be a mistake was either planned or spontaneous? No, it doesn't. This is because there are *no* mistakes in life. Sometimes our actions are planned and can be influenced by friends or society. Other times, we act spontaneously without thought. Whether our actions are spontaneous or planned doesn't matter, though, because however we choose to act at any given moment is the correct choice. Our reaction to a situation in the moment is our truth at that moment. We are expressing what we think is needed for a particular outcome to occur. Whether or not this outcome actually manifests is out of our control. We may not choose to act in the same way the next time, but we still shouldn't feel regret or reprimand ourselves over the choice we already made. Even if we see the outcome of an action we took as negative, our limited perspective makes it difficult to know, for sure, whether it's actually negative or not in the larger context of life.

So, it is very important to remember that one's truth in the moment should never be the cause for regret later. Living in truth helps to keep regret from forming. Regret is more likely to form and surface when we are deceiving ourselves and others. Does feeling regret help us to change our ways so that we can live more in truth? It does not. It only belittles us, causing us to feel wrong and inadequate. We must not have regret for anything we have done, even if it is terribly wrong, because truth is often revealed to us through the act of performing misdeeds. If we are slow learners, this process may continue for a while before we are ready to change. Will regret help to shorten this time? No. In fact, it tends to prolong the time, keeping us stuck in the past and causing us to re-create a similar event and outcome over and over.

Stop regretting your actions and accept that your decisions are perfect at each moment, for if they weren't, you would have chosen something else. Realize, also, that the next situation you face may call for a completely different decision, even if this new decision arises out of the previous action. In a significant way, this shows the continuous flow and spontaneity of life from one action to the next.

Many people have the opinion that regret is a valid emotion to experience. By regretting the past, they think they will come to new realizations that will allow them to see and do things differently in the future. Their real focus should be on *reflection*, however, because reflection is something very different from regret. Reflection is a contemplative process wherein one's intuitive wisdom is tapped into and awareness is used, instead of the mind, to bring forth realizations that positively affect their life. This is very different from wanting to change experiences that have occurred in the past. Reflection raises consciousness, whereas regret and guilt are detrimental and keep us glued to the past. If we want to move beyond this, we must go deep inside ourselves and use our expansive awareness to clearly see that a choice made in the past may no longer be beneficial now. Reflection raises our consciousness in a manner that helps us evolve.

True reflection comes from awareness. When we use the mind to focus on regret, excuses are made and delusions arise. But when we reflect using awareness, we pave the way for the manifestation of positive effects in our lives and the world.

Rejoice, for you are perfect, including all that you create. Just as God does not regret one single thing that was created, neither should you regret the decisions you make or the actions you take. Always remember that God created you, and in God's kingdom all is perfect.

Express Your Self

How can we express our Selves so that others will fully understand? Both expressing and understanding require an open mind. We all want to be understood, the problem is that we tend to enter a discussion with a closed mind. We are more concerned with getting our own view across than with listening to another person's view. This causes us to miss what others have to say, which is equally valid. We falsely believe that our ideas are our truths. We spend a lifetime gaining experience and knowledge so that we can tell others what we think about various subjects.

Sanity is based on a majority having common ideas about the world. When we have ideas different from the norm, others may consider us strange or even insane. Because we don't want to be considered strange, we often hide our true feelings. All of us have dark and indecent thoughts at times that we don't want others to know about. We hide this part of us so we will fit the image of a "normal person." Our true thoughts are given up so that we may be accepted and liked. Being accepted is what's most important to us, because society says we must "fit in." We then lose our individuality and our creativity. We watch every move we make to ensure that we are approved of by others. But when we do this, all of our energy is focused on who we should be, rather than *who we really are*. We may not be insane, but we are no longer in touch with our truth. Instead, we are only in touch with what we think others expect from us.

Our psyche, however, longs to be identified with its own fingerprints that say, "There is no one in the world quite like me. I am unique, and have my own distinct identity." We must draw from the uniqueness, which our fingerprints represent and be willing to declare, "I am who I am, and if you can't accept that...it's all right with me."

Self-expression is our natural form of communication. This means letting the world know who we really are. When we block Self-expression, we shut down our whole existence. We may think that to conform is best because it makes us feel secure. But what is security, if the price is losing our Soul? While we are alike and equal in many ways, we are also unique in other ways. To know that we are equals and come from the same Source is very important. This knowledge keeps us from judging others. But to also know that our individual expression is unique and there is no one else that exists in the present, past, or future who is exactly like us is equally important. It verifies the relevance of each individual's destiny.

Stop trying to fit in—it doesn't work. You are either too big or too small, never just the right size. Only when you compare your Self to your Self do you find your size perfect, your mind perfect, and your soul perfect. Instead of expending your energy on conforming, use it to learn how to express your True Self.

You have lost the words to express your true feelings and your true thoughts. You must get to know your Self once again so that the words you speak come from the truth held deep within you. Don't deny your Self this. There must be no false appearances or false deceptions; instead, there must be real actions and profound thoughts that enable your energy to flow in its correct direction. Your True Self needs to be exposed, and it craves to be heard, so your life's expression can be fully realized. Come forth with all you have to say—say it to me, to her, to him, to them. Don't worry if it's accepted or not, that's not important. If others don't agree when you reveal your inner truths, then listen to them carefully with an open heart, for your apparent truth could be a deception based on an idea. If so, you must acknowledge this and thank your Self for such an important realization and for being humble enough to admit the truth.

Most of us think we know everything and it is difficult to admit to our Selves that we actually know very little. We are not here to prove that we are right, however, but to see that what's right is different for everyone. In our own reality we are right, but who else lives in our reality besides our Selves? Of course, nobody does. So having an open heart removes this feeling of separateness. Your essence and everyone else's essence is the same. We are all equal in this way. Make room in your life to connect with many others, for then you will all share your views and learn from each other.

If you see that the truth isn't being told, it is your duty to make this known. You are here to help your Self and to help others. We are, ultimately, on the same boat together; if you let the boat sink, all of us will go down with it. If the waves come from truth, they will be calm. But if the waves come from deception, tidal waves will occur. You were given this body, mind, and soul to express your Self and to come forth in wholeness to make a difference. You have this life to make a difference, so share your truth by using your unique Self expression to paint reality. Your colors are shining through. Do you see them? They see you.

Who Am I?

Let's not ever forget to ask this question,
even if in our life it was never mentioned.
We come into life full of joy, strife, and apprehension,
but our joy does not need to ask this question,
why did we ever make this descension?
It is already full within itself
with happiness, love, and an abundance of nature's wealth.
And when we come to apprehension,
we automatically move into a different direction.
But it's our innocence that gives us a profound, innate strength within
to conquer all that we doubt, even the darkest sin.

It's strife that ultimately makes us think
why we were created, in an eye's quick blink.
This strife we so overtly hate and deny
takes us to a place where we can recognize
our true existence and its real size.
Without distress in our lives
we will not fully see and realize
that the shadows we own
are gifts to be felt and shown
to ourselves and everyone we have ever known.

For this is what brings us into wholeness
to the true awareness of our soulness.
So let's not ever stop asking this question: Who am I?
Because it's the basis of every thought that makes us ask why.

Healthy Dependency

Where does your dependency lie: in mankind, God, or yourself? All three are important for receiving the support and strength we need. But, it's acquiring a healthy balance of the three in our lives that leads to a fulfilling, meaningful existence. Each of us makes our own choice as to how much we rely on each.

Some of us go through life allowing others to make our decisions for us. This may appear convenient, but in reality, we lose our power and self-respect when we do this, which is difficult to live without. Or on the other hand, we choose to decide everything for ourselves and are deafened to advice from friends and family. Such an attitude often leads to self-righteousness and stubbornness, two difficult traits to live with. We may also decide that God's way is the only way and live life abiding diligently to religious rules, or by our own self-imposed spiritual beliefs. But this can result in dogmatic ideas and inflexibility.

Balancing our life is like being a tightrope walker, moving to one side slowly, with both feet gripping the rope. If one side of the body is leaning too far, even if ever so slightly, the weight will be unevenly distributed and the tightrope walker will fall. This skill of tightrope walking is not something one is born with; rather, it is a skill that needs to be developed and mastered throughout life. Similarly, balancing all three types of dependency, when each is called for, attains balance in our lives.

Humankind is our sister, our brother, and our heart connection. We are meant to support each other and to share the joy, pain, sorrow, grief, and ecstasy that we all experience in life. We cannot do this alone—for without having brothers and sisters, none of these sentiments would be felt, expressed, or even exist. It's two or more people interacting together that create the dynamics for this "dance of life." We must participate and experience relationship to the fullest. Each person we come into contact with is here to teach us something. These human interactions are a gift that must be received with open arms. They may not always be beautiful or kind, but each relationship helps us to see our self in a unique way and to develop our own potential more fully. We must be open to life's banquet and taste every dish that's been created. Only then can we select and pick what best suits our taste buds.

Our self-respect comes from the love we have for ourselves. We get little support for loving ourselves from our society. Western culture often downplays and trivializes our sense of self-worth, sending a message that we need materialistic possessions to feel worthy and powerful. If we truly loved ourselves, we wouldn't need half the things that society offers. Self-love creates self-sufficiency, and it makes us aware that our inner self is full of magnificent treasures. We must draw from these inner treasures and use them in our daily lives. To balance our lives and become professional tightrope walkers, we also must listen to the intuitive messages we receive. These messages are very meaningful and without them we would be lost. These days many of us feel separate and out of control. This is due to the lack of awareness we have of our inner truths and how to connect with them. Like a magician who makes something materialize from nothing, we must pull out and use the inner riches that each one of us possess. They have been left deep inside of us for so long that we have become unaware and unconcerned about how to make them appear. These inner riches are there to calm us during life's storms, bring light to dark problems, strengthen us in weak moments, and give us the courage to continue life when it seems overwhelming.

Trusting in God is an important source of strength and guidance in our lives. We all have our own ideas about God, but many times these ideas are biased and there is no way of confirming what is really true. We fight for God's truth, we kill for our beliefs, and we wage war over issues we think God stands for. Please tell me, why do we do this? Are we trying to convince ourselves that our beliefs are true? And we know that finding actual proof may be nearly impossible. Our religious or spiritual beliefs usually reflect our way of thinking, but we do not all think alike. So we must be open-minded and not force our views on others. God loves us all. He loves our *diversity*. Developing a personal relationship with God will help us to achieve balance and become a successful tightrope walker, for it will give us strength and connect us to our Source. This one-on-one relationship shows us that we need not fear God, that God does not judge us, and that we are considered equals in God's eyes.

Our quest in life is to find out who we really are and to connect with all of life. This broadens and deepens our balance. To achieve this, we must first have a loving relationship with ourselves. This means opening up to the truth of our being and accepting everything about ourselves. Healthy dependency also includes depending on our brothers and sisters for love and support. We must be flexible with others and love them like ourselves. We can listen and learn from them because they have had different life experiences than we have and can therefore teach us new things that we didn't know. And last, but not least, healthy dependency includes God, the One who created us. By finding a friend in God, we can talk to and share our life with God. We must let this friendship grow so that our reliance on God becomes as natural and comforting as that between best friends.

Being dependent in a healthy way on ourselves, humankind, and God is what will pull us through the void and into a spectrum of a vivid, colorful prism. This prism will carry us to the sun and back. So let your hearts be the pilot, your openness the passenger, and your convictions the route. Have a good take off and a safe journey!

On War and Violence

Is there any valid reason for war? Throughout the ages, mankind has insisted on using violence to resolve differences. Man has believed that by using force he could get what he wants. Indeed, force is a powerful weapon and we fear it because it destroys life, culture, and everything we have worked for. Wars are usually started for ludicrous reasons, such as religion (in the name of God), politics (what will I get out of it), money (how much will I make from it), and territory (this land belongs to me)–none of which are worthy enough to merit loss of life.

This belief in the validity of war continues today and is blindly accepted by most people. Even more absurd than this is the fact that soldiers are actually given honors for killing the most men or doing the greatest harm. During wars, soldiers often become like puppets without minds of their own, fighting someone else's battle. They don't think for themselves; instead, they follow the whims of a society who demands obedience, even if it's blind obedience. This is why many war veterans suffer psychologically and existentially after fighting a war—because it wasn't something they wholeheartedly chose to do. Orders were given that they felt must be obeyed, even if they disagreed, causing them to feel powerless. Wars are fought by the young, who most of the times have not yet found their inner power. They are easily brainwashed into believing that power can be attained by controlling and harming others.

So, who is to blame? Is it the one who gives the orders or the one who submits to them? We usually assume that the one who gives the orders is in full control and knows exactly what he is doing. However, he may be choosing to manipulate others to further his own ideology. Or he may be totally out of control, possessed by power, greed, and glory, which creates obsessive behavior. But then again, maybe war is the fault of the one who blindly submits and follows the orders, too weak to think for himself or too unaware to realize the real motives behind the war. It's as if the strong and the weak merge together to create a force that becomes one and the same. We cannot just blame our leaders for creating war. If we are willing to accept war and participate in it, then we, too, are to blame for it. The bottom line is: without us, war couldn't exist.

We must ask ourselves if there was really a leader killing innocent people without shame, such as Hitler, should he be left to commit these acts or should he be stopped? If a person in your city was going around killing people because he was mentally ill, would you let him continue? There have been many leaders in this world who have been mentally ill. Just because a person holds a position of authority, this should not stop us from questioning his decisions. Unfortunately, in our world today we place tremendous importance on having power. Whether a person has acquired their political power through inheritance, being appointed, or elected, often their decisions and actions are not questioned because of their prestigious position. Such blind acceptance cannot be tolerated any longer.

Can killing another human being ever be justified? Because each situation is unique, different points of view must be examined. From a realistic point of view, the philosophy "an eye for an eye and a tooth for a tooth" is revenge based and unacceptable. Yet many people today, in countries around the world, kill others based on this philosophy. Also unacceptable is the massacre of thousands of innocent people for the sake of creating a non-violent world. Yet this act, too, is justified by some as being honorable since the goal is the attainment of a non-violent world. Ponder this: if someone breaks into your home and attempts to kill your child, would you let your child be murdered or would you kill the perpetrator? Almost every parent in this situation would attempt to protect their child, even if it meant they had to kill to do this. So nothing is ever completely black and white in life because there are always so many *variables* to look at. Each situation is unique and must be given the respect it deserves, not labeled and judged by an inflexible belief system.

By the same token, each human being is unique and also deserves our respect. They should not be labeled and judged just because their beliefs differ from ours. It is important that we unite and live peacefully together, treating each other as equals. Anything that disrupts this unity cannot be overlooked anymore. We can not afford any longer to blindly give our power over to those who are in control of making life and death decisions for humanity. Now is the time to take responsibility for ourselves by voicing and acting on our own beliefs instead of letting others control our minds and hearts.

We must have the courage to follow our hearts. If something resonates intuitively as true, we can no longer ignore it. If someone tells us to fight a war because it's our duty, we must think about it carefully. Then we need to go even deeper into silence and feel the situation in our heart. Our heart always tells the truth. If our truth is to fight in a war because we wholeheartedly believe that it will help humankind, then God is with us. For in God's eyes there is no right or wrong—this type of thinking is dogmatic and shallow. In God's view, the only valid actions are those which are based on deep and honest feelings. These feelings are different for everyone. God accepts all of these different choices, as long as the choice is *true to you*, and not the choice of another.

Expanding Love

Love has various levels of meaning. It can refer to physical love, or on a more profound level, it can be a deep feeling of benevolence for everyone we encounter. Whether it is our lover, best friend, sister, schoolmate, stranger, or enemy, we treat everyone with equal benevolence.

Normally, our feelings of love do not extend much beyond the boundary of family, where we are bonded by blood, beliefs, and physical traits. Are these the only reasons why we should love someone? Or should we consider every living thing as a part of our family? Our family must extend outwards to every living soul. Why do we limit family to our brothers and sisters, sons and daughters? Is it because relating to our nuclear family is "the known" and gives us a feeling of security? Know that our love is capable of expanding further than our biological family—it can touch every soul with whom we come into contact. This is nonjudgmental and unconditional love. You don't have to be married to a person or even have the same blood to love them, you only need to be part of the same human race—this is enough.

Do you think I loved only the monks that worshipped under my name? And do you think God only loves those who listen to him? *Exclusion* is not a word that exists in God's dictionary. Everyone is loved, no matter how they live. How much we are able to accept and love each other is the barometer for how evolved our soul really is. What a wonderful feeling that arises within us when we are friendly to everyone we meet and offer help to anyone who needs it. One may adopt a child, give money to the needy, volunteer services to the underprivileged, donate goods to the starving, pray for everyone to be happy, visualize a healthy planet, and ask that war may stop, for our human family lives in every part of this world.

Let's open our arms wide so that we can include all of our enemies, all that we're prejudiced against, all races, and all religions. We should do away with nationalities and become citizens of the world, where we were all born. We must destroy the borders that separate us from one another. Our world must become *one* world that unites us and enables us all to experience a life of opportunity, abundance, and equality: a life everyone of us deserves. If these beneficial circumstances are lacking in even one part of the world, then we are not living this truth. We must lift the oppression that denies so many people freedom and we must grant everyone the opportunity to live in abundance and harmony. Our help is what's needed. Let's not turn our cheek the other way in apathy. Instead, let our hearts create an atmosphere of equality and justice for all living beings.

I know this has been said over and over, but who is really listening? Very few people listen, for if it is the least bit inconvenient, or time consuming, or costs us money, it is ignored. Please don't let this continue. Our generosity is the main ingredient to ending deprivation. Every open heart is naturally generous and every open mind understands that giving is our nature. Let's not give to just a select few, but to everyone in the whole universe, because they are also part of our family.

Natural Disasters

Why do natural disasters occur and why are we experiencing so many now? In the time in which we are currently living, there will be many natural disasters. When such disasters occur, we must pray for all the people who are suffering. This will raise the energy on earth and help to lessen both physical and mental destruction. The more energy we are able to give to the victims, the more benefit everyone will receive.

It's important to take time every day to bless every living thing in the world, and to make a wish that there may be balance and harmony on earth. We must not feel helpless or hopeless, for this only leads to apathy and stagnation. We must realize that our participation through prayer and other positive acts is very important. These acts can minimize the gravity of each natural disaster and help raise global consciousness, transforming the world.

The beginning of the new millennium means not only the beginning of a new century, but also a change in world consciousness. This change includes every living thing, from an ant to a serial killer. We must now begin to look at both the ant and the serial killer differently. Instead of stomping them, either with our foot or through capital punishment, we must try to understand their purpose in life and show compassion instead of disdain for them. No one has the right to take the life of any thing or anybody. The act of killing is born out of fear and ignorance. There is a reason for everything that exists in our great web of life. It is time for us to embrace the qualities of love and compassion. It is also time for us to develop everything which unites life. We must stop expending our energy on that which destroys life.

Our love for ourselves and others has been scarred and beaten, like a battered child. The injustices in our lives must not inhibit the deep love we have within us from shining through. Love is the greatest weapon we have and it protects us from all the hate that exists. We can no longer fight hate with hate. Tell me, has it worked in the past? It only seems to have increased our hatred, even for ourselves.

The earth cannot tolerate anymore hate, it's at its full limit. It must do whatever it can to survive. Because of our hate and disrespect for nature and ourselves, negative energy dominates our planet. This negative energy is contributing to the occurrence of these natural disasters. These disasters are nature's way of releasing and cleansing this negative energy. They will continue, I assure you, unless we change our way of thinking and begin to show more love for each other and the earth. We can no longer live ignoring our brothers and sisters or our planet earth, because nature *won't* let us. It is forcing us to reassess our values and commit ourselves to love, not hate. There is no more time for procrastination. We must embrace our *earth family*, from China to Africa and from Indonesia to Russia. Their suffering is our suffering; their loss is our loss. Let our compassion warm and console each victim, for tomorrow we may be the victims. That's how closely connected we all are.

I beg you all to open your hearts and let love flow out. In this kind of work, no one is unemployed. Each person brings his own unique loving energy that creates a bond of caring and oneness, uniting all living things. Be thankful for living in this momentous time. Your loving contribution confirms your commitment to world peace and equality.

I root you on like a spectator at a football match. My work is only to encourage you to live the *truth*, and nothing more.

Planetary Alignment

What does the alignment of the planets represent in this new millennium we are now living in? These planetary alignments mark mankind's opening to the energy of the cosmos that is so instrumental for our evolution. Such energy brings with it a different vibration than what has previously existed on earth. Furthermore, it provides us with the opportunity to enter the cosmic dimension more quickly than before. Such events are a gift from the cosmos that will help transform our existence so that we may finally live in love and peace.

This does not mean that everything in the future will be perfect. There will still be many changes on the planet, caused by natural disasters, war, and oppression. Increasingly, however, people are examining these negative situations more closely, enabling them to better understand their significance and to take more appropriate action.

Our increased awareness and openness is crucial in creating a new world order that recognizes the equality of all people. The understanding that our actions *do* result in reactions will cause us to think more clearly before we act. Our feelings of responsibility to the world will grow, enabling us to help determine the evolution of the planet. Our compassion will be sparked, making loving and accepting each other easier. The act of giving will come from the heart instead of being motivated by what one might get in return. The over abundance of resources in one area will be distributed more evenly to other areas so that there'll be less starvation.

This new increased awareness and openness that many are experiencing is the direct result of the shifting planetary alignments. The opportunity to be a part of this transformation is knocking at our door. Open it, our calling is now! There are no more deterrents holding us back from this deeply rewarding mission. Our evolved partners from the other realms, who share the heavens with us, have opened the skies to the eternal truths which have always existed. These truths have a vibration that is now shining on our planet. Earth's destiny has taken a turn for the better and it is our responsibility to implement these truths. There is no longer room for apathy or self-centeredness. Our past has shown that these only divide us.

Let your highest and deepest Being be revealed, so you may live life to the fullest. This is your mission now—it's not impossible; instead, it is deeply rewarding. May your soul push you beyond all limits to where you are *limitless*.

Why Terrorism?

To understand terrorism, we need to realize that there are always reasons why things happen—nothing is a coincidence and nothing is an accident—not even terrorism.

We must begin to realize that all of us in the world, at least to some degree, are participating in terrorism. Our priorities and what we value in life have gone astray. The desire for power that drives our political leaders has corrupted every facet of life. Every country is involved in this "hunger for power" and attains it through the use of manipulation, greed, suppression, oppression, stealing, and killing. These acts of overt and covert violence have become common in today's world. Money is considered more powerful than God, and this idea is crumbling our societies.

We must not make the mistake of believing that these acts of violence are only perpetuated by other nations but not our own. Instead, we must look within ourselves and our nation and take responsibility for our own corruption. Only when we do this can we actually begin to change things.

Each nation's disrespect and arrogance towards other cultures and religions are causing segregation and inequality. Most countries believe that their country is the best. But there is "no best" in the world because God has made all of us equal. This equality unites all human beings and it unites all nations, from America to Afghanistan.

To retaliate acts of violence with yet more violence never resolves anything. Retaliation only creates more warring and greater loss of life. It is a desperate act that only provides a temporary solution, like applying a bandage over a wound.

The wound does not heal from the bandage, though, but from the healing process that takes place within the body. Like the wound, our bodies and spirits also need to be healed. This cannot be done if we harbor hate and revenge, for this only creates more hate. Only love can heal our desperate nations; only love can mend our aching hearts.

The suffering that's being felt now, by many people, is the suffering of the world. Every nation has experienced fighting and oppression and many nations are experiencing ongoing wars. These conflicts create great suffering, but it is the feeling of separation that exists within ourselves and towards others that is the real cause of suffering.

We must raise our awareness and see clearly the futility of terrorism and war. Only then can we end the causes of them once and for all in our own lives. Our purpose on this planet is not to wage war on our brothers and sisters, but rather to open our hearts so that our love can be felt in every part of the world. Let our love open up new borders in our thinking process. Let us bless not just people in our own country, but people across the world.

We must hope that societies around the world will learn the real message that terrorism is giving us. If everyone on the planet opened themselves to *love*, there would be no terrorism or war. We mustn't feel discouraged or angry over these acts of terrorism, for this only increases their negative effects. Instead, we need to join together, not in a patriotic way, but in a human way, to send our love and our prayers to those who perpetrate these acts of violence.

Our obligation is to break through our own barriers of judgment and discrimination in order to realize that the tragedies of terrorism have a deep message for all of us. This message exists to reveal to us the dire consequences of judgment, inequality, and hate, which we harbor within ourselves and which we express towards others. These negative traits are what separate us from our fellow human beings and what causes tremendous suffering for ourselves and our world. Only when we heal these traits within us can we begin to heal them outside of us. *This is our work.* Our duty is to come forth and display the positive qualities of love, kindness, tolerance, patience, and generosity. It's time to show the world our true colors and intertwine these colors together to create the biggest, brightest, and most beautiful rainbow that has ever existed.

Fighting Terrorism

In order to truly fight terrorism we must first discover its roots hidden inside ourselves. Terrorism is born out of fear, paranoia, and a sense of self-righteousness. If we truly want to rid the planet of terrorism, we must first rid ourselves of these negative aspects. It is our own fears, paranoia, and self-righteousness that create an environment conducive to terrorism. If we want to create peace on earth we must first become "peace" ourselves. By shifting ourselves from being fearful to being loving and peaceful, we also shift the world. Only an act of this magnitude will end terrorism and all other acts of violence towards each other and ourselves.

Many of us were born at this particular time in history to help make this shift in consciousness. This is an exciting moment in the evolution of humankind because we are the ones chosen to implement this change.

It is important to realize that every contribution towards healing the world from terrorism and war is indispensable. Every one of us holds the key to the destiny of our life and our home—Planet Earth—and each of us can swing the pendulum from destruction to peace. It's a responsibility that we cannot ignore since our planet's survival is at stake.

We must look at this time in history as a time of great healing for the world. The darkness will dissipate as the light appears, but this will only happen if humankind works together in unity towards this goal. Each one of us must help by finding peace and light within ourselves and then letting it shine out into our world. Because the amount of light that shines through is inversely proportional to the amount of destruction there will be on earth, it is essential that we use this light now for the healing of the earth.

Ending terrorism in the world is dependent on first ridding ourselves of our own negative aspects, because here are the roots of terrorism. The more we can tear down the walls around our hearts, the more light will shine through. These walls are blocking us from knowing our true selves. Although we have built these walls, innocently, to protect ourselves from the pain of everyday life, they actually hurt us. They block our access to our essential qualities of love and joy. Knowing this, we must make a conscious effort to open our hearts, because it rarely seems to happen on its own. We must be disciplined and diligently spend twenty minutes each day concentrating on opening our hearts (see visualization to *Opening the Heart*, Chapter 2).

When you feel your heart is open, you can then channel your positive qualities into healing yourself, humanity, and the earth. Respect every living thing and share your love with all life, even if what you see appears to be your enemy. This visualization to open your heart can be even more effective when done in a group. These groups should include children, too, for they need support in this effort to keep all hearts open. The unification of many loving hearts for the purpose of peace and love on earth is stronger than any bomb. It is the strongest medicine we have to heal hate.

May your love shine through to create a ray of light that will glow throughout the hemisphere and grow into an energy where only *peace* prevails on Earth.

Sweet Surrender

Sweet, sweet surrender, this sentiment that fills our body
with deep trust;
trust that life is perfect;
trust that our life is unfolding exactly the way it is meant to,
even though it may not seem so;
trust that our pain and sorrow will help us to understand
compassion, and give us strength to move forward;
trust that God's view expands way beyond ours, seeing the
completion and totality in everything;
trust that our small self can move mountains, if we are
determined enough;
trust that God's arms are long enough to embrace each
and every one of us;
trust that God's love is omnipresent, so we may draw from it whenever
our hearts feel empty;
trust that we will be forgiven each time we hurt ourselves
or any one else;
trust that the more we surrender to the Holy Spirit, the less
fears we'll have;
trust that when we ask wholeheartedly, we shall receive
wholeheartedly;
trust that what we put out is what we get back;
trust that the injustices that haunt our faith in God have a higher pur-
pose and a higher meaning;
trust that when our bodies pass away, our souls are here to stay;
trust that we are never, ever alone, but loved infinitely by God and
connected profoundly to every living thing;
trust that we are all one big happy family and that earth is our beauti-
ful happy home;
trust that our surrender to God will awaken us,
awaken us to the remembrance of the oneness,

the remembrance of the oneness we share with God, the oneness we share with every living thing;
trust that the bond we have created is strong, so strong that we will never feel separate or alone again.

What does it take to surrender all you have? What does it take to risk all you have? Yes! It takes all you have and even more to surrender yourself to God, to surrender right now, and to see that it's worth more than you could ever imagine. So just trust my words, trust in God, and surrender yourself sweetly to this incredible, ecstatic energy. You'll lose only that which you don't like in yourself, and gain all that you want in yourself.

Transforming Sickness to Health

When we hear the word sickness, what comes to mind? Perhaps an old person in the hospital dying of a stroke, or a friend's father who died unexpectedly of a heart attack, or maybe even a school mate who has a brain tumor, or a cousin who has AIDS, or a little child who has leukemia. Sickness does not spare any age group. It is a reminder that any one of us, at any time, could be struck with an illness. Why does this happen so often? What does it mean?

Our bodies are a *reflection* of our state of mind. Our thoughts actually manifest physically as the emotions and feelings that we experience. We first have a thought, and then an emotion arises from it. We live our lives fluctuating from one emotion to the next and this causes us to become prisoners of our own emotions. We can no longer see the truth in our situations, or the larger picture, because we are stuck in whatever emotion has come over us. Our actions arise out of our emotional states and, most of the time, we don't think about how emotions control us because it seems so normal. But it isn't normal. We are actually meant to be free—mentally, physically, emotionally, and spiritually.

Such freedom does not mean allowing the mind to indulge in any thought or emotion it desires. It means being mindful of each thought, so that we are conscious instead of unconscious. We have the innate ability to distinguish which thoughts are positive and which ones are negative, but we tend to forget this. We let ourselves get drawn into, and identify with, sentiments that harm us and break down our immune system. We are addicted to the emotional dramas of our lives.

And like a drug without the adrenaline rush created by the drama, we feel our life has no meaning. Most of us live like the soap operas we watch on TV. We pollute our minds with too much trivial stimulation because, subconsciously, we want to numb ourselves so that we don't have to deal with the real meaning of our life. Our hopes of life's great potential degenerate into mere survival tactics, creating adrenaline rushes to excite the body. Our principles and values have become tainted. We now idolize the rich, famous, and powerful, instead of respecting and emulating someone like the Dalai Lama who is a constant example of love, wisdom, and compassion in action. We do not care anymore about discovering who we really are. Instead, we focus on how we look or on the possessions we have. All of this is making us sick, sicker, and sickest.

Our bodies cannot handle the physical, mental, and emotional junk that we are feeding them. We are infested with toxins that break down our immune systems, allowing diseases to attack us. We are living in a manner that is contrary to health. We must allow sickness to teach us that the guilt, hate, anger, jealousy, and fear we experience in our minds find a place in our bodies. We must learn that when they are held there and digested, they make us ill. These feelings must be confronted and dealt with as soon as they are felt, for they are the real "killers" of our century. They cannot be ignored any longer. When negative feelings arise, we must learn to identify them, sit with them in silence, and honor them until they no longer have a hold on us. Only when we consciously acknowledge them and feel them deeply will they dissolve and be replaced with our essential qualities of love, compassion, and joy. This is how true healing occurs.

Our world is falling apart. Our environment is polluted. Countries are fighting each other. Societies are competing against one another. Our schools are rampant with violence. Our neighborhoods are divided. Our homes are divorced. Our brothers are our enemies and we are separated from our True Selves. If we wish to reverse this, we must start with ourselves and become whole again. We must ask, "What is it we are deeply feeling? What creates our feelings of separation, despair, and anger?" Ask yourself these questions and then go even deeper. Keep asking, and don't stop until an answer comes forth. If you cannot find an answer, pray for help from God who is always willing and waiting. We cannot ignore the sickness in the world any longer. We need everyone's help to heal the world. If you are not healthy yourself, then how can you help anyone else to become healthy? Sickness excludes no one, so we must together make a commitment to heal the planet by healing ourselves.

Take the sickness you may have, be it small or big, and open your heart to it. It is your savior, it is your teacher, and it is telling you the truth by personalizing the dynamics of your life. Each and every one of us gets sick, so don't feel alone. Our life is like a puzzle filled with many different experiences. When we put these different experiences together, they create the whole of our life. You must look at where your puzzle cracks have manifested. And you must love each piece and every crack, because this puzzle represents your uniqueness as an individual. This is beautiful, and you are beautiful, even with every flaw you have. You must honor your flaws and have the strength and courage to look at them deeply. Your weaknesses of the past can be your strengths in the future. Without them, you are not whole. Let your wholeness manifest, for only then will love, happiness, and health prevail.

The Grieving Process

The grieving process is such a natural avenue for growth and health, but we have forgotten how to use it. We are conditioned by society to believe that displaying too much pain is not acceptable and that it makes us appear weak and vulnerable. So we hide our true feelings, pushing them away when the urge to release them arises. We have become a society of "silent grievers." The irony of concealing these emotions is that grieving is meant to be shared with others as part of the process.

Grieving stems from the lack of trust we have in life, in death, and in God. If we truly believed that our life is in perfect order no matter what happens, and that all is God's creation, our sense of trust and surrender would eliminate much of our grieving. If we saw death as a passage from one life to another, and realized that we lose only the body and that our soul has eternal life, the grief we feel would lessen tremendously.

Our doubts concerning who we are and what actually happens to us after death are what create our deep feeling of fear, emptiness, despair, and pain. When we lose someone or something dear to us, these feelings are magnified because it reminds us of our *own* mortality and brings to the surface our repressed fear of death. Many of us stop ourselves from grieving because we want to deny this fear that feels so overwhelming. Doing this, however, is not taking responsibility for our lives. Because we deny ourselves the natural expression of grief, we feel stifled and depressed and tend to blame others for our misery.

Another equally negative scenario is when we become obsessed with grieving. In this case, we continue to grieve indefinitely for fear that we will lose the connection we have with our loved one. A person who reacts like this is unable to accept the loss and long term suffering is often the result. Both repressing our grief or becoming obsessed with it is equally unhealthy and harmful.

We must learn to value and fully express grief. This is important because it confirms that life's pains and losses contribute to our wisdom and wholeness. Moreover, by surrendering completely to grief, we are free to experience its opposite—*full rejoicing*. We are able to rejoice fully when we are able to grieve fully. Having grieved fully, we are then able to celebrate having had our precious loved one in our life. We can celebrate the relationship we shared together, the growth we experienced from having known them, the deep connection we felt to them, the love we gave to one another, and the acceptance we received from each other. The memories and love that we are left with after the death of a loved one will always be with us, for our loved ones never die in spirit. This is why we rejoice, for without these special connections with people and animals, our lives would be empty and meaningless.

There must always be a beginning, a middle, and an end to grieving. The beginning starts when we are willing to open our hearts to the loss we feel inside, the middle is when we are able to share and express that loss, and the end is when we can surrender to and accept the loss. Each part of this process takes an enormous amount of courage. It is this courage, which all of us have, that enables us to move forward from one part to the next, until all the parts are touched and the process is complete.

Let's not forget that "process" is the key to every issue that exists in life. It's our dedication to the process that determines the outcome. We can either choose to move forward, taking risks and living with zest, or we can fall back, being afraid to take each step and living in fear of our own shadow. The latter choice creates only despair, while the prior choice takes us to a place where joy, gratitude, and love prevail.

Channeling

What does this word "channeling" actually mean? To understand the significance of channeling, let's compare it to watching television. People usually watch TV to be entertained or informed. However, unlike in the past when TV programs were more entertaining and meaningful, today the potential value of TV has been lost. It is now primarily used for making money and anesthetizing the masses. Often, it programs us to be like zombies, destroying our ability to think for ourselves—or even to think at all.

By contrast, when we are involved in the ancient form of communication called channeling, we are not being controlled by greed, manipulation, or violence. Instead, we are receiving information transmitted by spirits, motivated to help the evolution of mankind. Like an antenna picking up TV signals, waves of energy are passed from one entity to another. If people are open—that is, if they have their TV on—they can easily become a channel.

Just like choosing a program you can relate to, these transmitting spirits purposefully contact people able to understand and accept their messages. These spirits will often come to a person who is asking for guidance, which is why they are known as "spirit guides." Then, like the TV guide, they will direct you to where help and guidance is needed.

Anyone who is attracted to connecting with spirit guides can simply turn on their TV, get relaxed, and ask to be contacted. Be sure to request the highest and most positive entity available. It may take a while, but be persistent. People who ask to be contacted, but aren't, may be trying too hard. This can block communication. Just be patient, open, and keep on asking, because at some point you will be contacted if you want to be. Remember to not be doubtful and to accept that this phenomenon is actually quite common. This attitude can help channeling to occur faster.

It is important to be open and stay centered. You may be contacted in a subtle way through the use of thoughts or feelings, or in an obvious way through the use of voices, colors, sounds, or writing. All of these are different modes used in channeling and are valid and meaningful. Don't be afraid if you feel negative energy, just ask it to go away, and it will. Your positive and loving intention for wanting this information will keep the process pure.

Sometimes these guides may appear without warning on your mental TV screen and start a conversation. At first your mind may think it's a figment of your imagination. But as time goes by and the experience of channeled communication becomes more common, you will realize that the information you are receiving is both profound and useful.

In addition to providing useful and inspiring information, channeling's main objective is to help you in your search for truth. Since it represents a vital connection to the non-physical spirit world, making contact with spirit guides is further proof that there is life after death.

Don't be afraid to use this form of communication. By not switching on this rich alternative to TV, you will miss one of the most *pertinent* information sources available in this age.

Evaluating Belief Systems

Our belief system is meant to be like a mirror reflecting our ideas about life. But sometimes the reflection can be tarnished by such influences as parents, school, peers, and society. These influences often condition and impose their particular belief systems on us, even though they may not correspond to what we actually believe. We don't question them, though, because they come from such strong influences in our life. Unfortunately, many people today feel powerless and alienated from themselves because they are letting others decide their life's issues for them. It is time to re-examine our beliefs and decide if they are true or not.

Our belief systems are always being challenged because new ideologies are constantly appearing. It is our *self-awareness* that directs us to what is true for us. If our self-awareness is not developed, it is easy to fall under the influence of outside forces. Not developing our self-awareness is one of the main reasons for the unhappiness and confusion people are currently experiencing. This is especially true for our teenagers. As parents, we tend to forget that our children have their own identities and belief systems. When we impose our ideas on them, we create a volatile situation. They feel that they must either rebel—which alienates our children from us, or submit—which steals their soul away from themselves. As parents, we are not here to hinder their growth, but rather to facilitate it. Our children have a right to choose the appropriate path for themselves.

Our schools are breeding clones that think and act alike; instead, they should be encouraging our children to think for themselves so that they can develop brilliant minds and evolve to higher realms of consciousness. It's important that we give our children reasons to respect their elders and view them as wise and knowledgeable. We must not allow our own fears of the unknown to keep our children from creating new realities and new ways of thinking. We must give our children the respect that's due them, for they will be the innovators and founders of a new world. Hopefully, the world they create will be more intelligent and sane than the one we're living in now. We need our children's input in order to evolve.

We are rapidly becoming a race without hopes and aspirations, a race that is regressing instead of evolving. Our natural impulse is to evolve and to create, but belief systems that are based on old and worn out beliefs are holding us back. We must face the truth of our circumstances and become more self-aware, or we will annihilate ourselves and our planet.

By having the courage to sincerely look at our beliefs and evaluate each one, we can learn to become more self-aware. It is our self-awareness that will enable us to determine the truth within ourselves. To accomplish this, it is crucial that we become silent and introspective at times. Only when we are silent and introspective will we become more self-aware and capable of developing a belief system that is based on a higher and more evolved consciousness.

What is Perfection?

Is perfection a state of mind,
or is it physical beauty?
Is it something we can see,
or is it only our imagination?

Is it a thought we create,
or does it already exist?
Is it a form we aspire to be,
or are we already born with it?

Is it an idea that we find frightening,
or do we embrace it graciously?
Is it in our every day life,
or is it far off in paradise?

Is it the waves that break on the beach,
or is it the beach that the waves break on?
Is it the air we breath,
or is it the lungs that breath the air?

Is it the tree that shades us from the sun,
or is it the sun that provides us light?
Is it the flowers that bloom in the spring,
or is it the spring that turns gracefully into summer?

Is it the stars that twinkle in the sky,
or is it the moon that influences our moods?
Is it the wind that blows the leaves to the ground,
or is it the rain that gives us water to drink?

Is it the birds that fly so high,
or is it the snakes that crawl so low?

Is it the eyes that see these things,
or is it the hands that touch them?

Is it the mind that can rationalize,
or is it the heart that can feel?
Is it the soul that understands perfection,
or is it only God that truly understands it?

Are we perfection made in the image of God,
or are we limited like a world without hope?
Can we still save the world and life's perfections,
or have we destroyed them with our greed,
indulgence, and power?

Has our soul been ignored for so long
that it no longer exists?
Look deep inside and tell me,
What is perfection?

Dear Disappointment

Would we be happier and more fulfilled in life without disappointments? No, but usually we think that we would because there is a false assumption about what disappointment represents. When disappointment floods your heart you may think, "Why did this happen to me? Did I cause this terrible outcome to happen or was it something that was inevitable regardless of how I acted?" Such responses are natural and healthy, for to examine why disappointment occurs is to examine the causes and effects in life. And although no one likes the feeling of disappointment, it does exist for a purpose.

The dictionary describes "to disappoint" as to fail to fulfill the hope or expectation of something. We often believe that hope and expectation are unworthy feelings because they can result in us being let down. If we truly believe this, though, then these two words are stripped of their potential. In reality, *hope* and *expectation* are what keeps our lives in motion. Often we say, "Oh, if only I hadn't expected or hoped for that, I wouldn't be feeling so disappointed now." But this is not so. It would be truer to say that if we would have had greater hope for it, if we had totally expected it, it probably would have happened. Truly, it is because we do not hope wholeheartedly, because we hold back due to our fear of possible disappointment, that events are often kept from happening.

Disappointment is not negative; rather, it is necessary for growth because it helps us to gain a better perspective on life. Without disappointment, our lives would become stagnant. Without disappointment, we would have little motivation to better ourselves or to really examine what our real needs are. Disappointment humbles us by letting us know that whatever we expected to achieve didn't work out the way we hoped that it would. We then usually ask the question, "Why?" This is what motivates us to re-examine our motives, actions, and dreams. Through deep introspection, we are able to discover what's really important to us. Disappointment also keeps us from becoming arrogant, because each time we are disappointed we become more vulnerable and more open.

The feeling of *elation* is the other side of disappointment. Without feeling disappointment, we could not experience elation. Only by experiencing both of them in our lives do we become more balanced. When one emotion is accepted but its opposite is not, the result is disharmony. This disrupts mankind and nature, causing sickness and even natural disasters. We must always accept both contrasting emotions, for they were created equally to maintain harmony in the world.

Additionally, we must allow disappointment to teach us the meaning of true despair. It is only when we are at the bottom of the valley that we have the opportunity to climb back up the mountain strong and full of vigor, ready to learn and grow with each new obstacle that appears in front of our path. Such so-called "obstacles" play an important role in our lives. They will remain until they no longer serve us. When we truly realize who we are and no longer need these tools of disappointment to help us discover this, they will in a sense disappear. It's not that disappointing things won't happen, it's just that the feeling of being disappointed will no longer be our response. Disappointment will cease to exist as we presently know it, except as a memory of how it once felt. We will have then truly reached a new level of awareness.

Self-Empowerment

The word power has many various connotations for each of us. In today's world, however, the most prevalent is the "abuse of power." This abuse has changed the word power from meaning positive strength to implying dishonesty and corruption. We see this abuse of power being used in all walks of life: by politicians, by religious leaders, and by everyday folk.

True power comes from our innate wisdom and is used for self-expression and creativity. Everyone must decide for themselves how to utilize their power. It can be used to enhance lives or to destroy them. We can learn from others who have misused their power to avoid making the same mistakes. To do this, it is crucial that we see the difference between egotistic power, which is self-centered and often becomes abusive, and our own real inner power, which is our divine birthright.

It is important that we are constantly mindful of our intentions. If we see that we are using our power in a negative way, we must have the strength of character to stop. When we see that we are using our inner power to express truth, we are using our power in a positive way that helps all of mankind. Each one of us possesses our own special talents and qualities, which is our way of expressing our truth. Expressing our truth is an example of true power.

For this reason, it is important that each person discovers what special talents they have to develop. What is yours? What have you always dreamed of doing but did not have the courage to try? What makes you feel so good when you're doing it that you feel like you could explode? The answers to these questions are what you should empower. With this done, your energy will rise to levels you have never felt before.

Don't compromise yourself by accepting a job you don't really want or a lifestyle that's not feeding your soul. We are not here to compromise, but to challenge ourselves to levels that are unimaginable. When we live in opposition to our true nature, we are going against God's plans for us. Compromising ourselves is not our natural state and only leads to depression. Depression is a state of mind that is trying to relay an important message to us. If only we would listen, it is telling us that it's time to shift our perceptions or to change our circumstances. Our habitual thoughts and living patterns create a parasitic situation that consumes our energy and limits our power to create. We are creative beings and are not meant to stagnant. We must continually evolve by accepting new challenges and taking risks. We must not just show up for our performance in life, but should perform with all the power and energy we possess.

God is watching with enthusiasm and giving us all the *support* necessary for success. Let's listen carefully so that we can hear God rooting for us loudly, so loudly that the sound actually amplifies the strength we have inside us. We can then share this power with our brothers and sisters and encourage them to share their power, as well. By working together, we will empower each other to strive for unlimited creativity and excellence based on our individual talents. True self-empowerment is when we compassionately root our fellow human beings on so that everyone receives the standing ovation they deserve.

Illusions of Control

It's the "illusion" that keeps us adrift—the illusion that we are just the body and our life only has meaning in the physical, material world. This illusion carries us to a plane of fear creating a sense of separation which stifles us. It keeps us from focusing on who we really are and the true meaning of our existence. Instead of moving with the flow of life, we are swept back with the tide, fearing that the swim to Paradise Island is unattainable. So we build a raft to keep us afloat, neither wanting it to pull us too far out or too close in. We are happy we have this raft, for it seems to protect us from the dangers of this ocean. If the raft starts to sway or tip over, we hold on to it for dear life. No one wants to fall off, but the ocean isn't always tranquil. It has storms, squalls, hurricanes, and typhoons that can't be controlled. We want to believe that we can control nature, but we are only creating the illusion of control and this false creation only contributes to our feeling of separation and alienation.

Like the ocean, we are a part of nature. Our body and mind are influenced by the cycles of the tides, seasons, and stars that we cannot control. Life is unpredictable, and the notion that we can control it to gain security is simply not true.

We humans are on the earth like dolphins are in the ocean, fulfilling nature's quest for perfection. But while a dolphin moves with each current, following its natural rhythm, humans often resist the natural flow. Trying to control the currents keeps us from realizing our innate power and from pursuing our intended destiny. We believe that we are more evolved than other species and have used our rational mind to create a sophisticated technology that attempts to control nature. But our technology is annihilating our environment which can only work against our evolution.

Conquering and abusing nature is resulting in slow suicide for the human race. We have lost our connection to our True Self and our relationship with Mother Earth. Although we have created a powerful new world where computers reign supreme, we will never have the power to control nature. All of this should be more than enough to remind us how we are actually meant to live on this planet, which is naturally and in harmony with nature.

Our path isn't difficult, it's our illusions that make it seem so. But rather than trying to conquer nature, we must look to her for help in simplifying our life. Nature doesn't have an ego. Its beauty, wholeness, and connection with everything are expressed spontaneously. By observing other living forms, we can learn how easily life can be lived. So let's destroy our illusions rather than destroying nature, because our illusions are our true enemies. Instead, let's befriend all life forms and learn from each of them how to live spontaneously. And let's give thanks to the Almighty Force, who from compassion created nature's perfection as a model for us to realize our own perfection. Let's not take nature or ourselves for granted any longer, for *we* and *nature* are *one*.

Suffering

Is suffering necessary for the development of our spirituality? Actually, suffering was never intended to exist on earth. It has been used by religions as a mechanism to control behavior and viewed as necessary for the development of spirituality. People are taught that they must "earn the right" to have a relationship with God through suffering. This philosophy is based on the premise that the more pain we experience in this lifetime, the greater our chances are for entrance into heaven and enjoying freedom in the afterlife. This belief makes us think that suffering is a worthy cause, but in truth, it only perpetuates itself.

I, myself, lived a life full of mental and physical suffering. I felt unworthy of happiness because I believed if Jesus suffered so much in life, then I too must follow his way. I learned, however, that the suffering I chose was futile. How could Jesus have suffered if he is total love? Love does not include suffering.

The positive result of suffering that we sometimes see is that it often causes us to become more vulnerable and open. This can help us to break down the walls we keep around us for protection, enabling us to delve deeper into the truth of our existence. It can open our hearts so that we can empathize more easily with others and be compassionate. However, suffering isn't the only way to achieve these results. There are other more positive options that we can use, such as special techniques that open the heart and allow us to experience compassion. These techniques are just as effective and they are less harmful (see the visualization in chapter 2, *Opening the Heart*).

If we were taught the truth—that suffering is an invalid response—it would eventually lose both its power and its hold on us. Unfortunately, our religions keep suffering burning in our hearts by teaching us that it is important and inevitable. It may seem so, but this isn't completely true. There are people who don't suffer and they are considered to be true Enlightened Beings. Such Beings accept each action and consequence in their life with trust, no matter how difficult it appears to be. They realize that within this human existence there is always pain. Pain is included in love, but suffering is not. Suffering is created by our *resistance* to pain. Without our resistance to pain, there would be no suffering.

People who are afflicted with an illness, be it mental or physical, or who have been the recipient of a violent action, are the ones who seem to suffer the most. Because of the tremendous pain they feel, it is not easy to tell such people that suffering is not necessary. They must accept their pain, however, for only then does it lose its intensity and allows them to see more clearly the deeper cause of it.

Our souls choose particular illnesses or acts of violence so that we can further evolve. By understanding the issues in our life that are at the root of our supposed misfortunes, we are able to move forward more easily. If we could view these unwanted circumstances as opportunities to discover deeper aspects of ourselves, instead of fearing and hating them, then much of the suffering we experience would dissipate. Inadvertently, this shift in perspective may even positively change the circumstance in our life and the suffering may cease. Our fear of death, life, love, failure, poverty, violence, war, and so much more, perpetuates this suffering. The *acceptance* of life itself and all the circumstances in it is how to eradicate suffering. Trusting that there is a purpose in the higher scheme of life for everything that happens shows us that these circumstances are often necessary for our growth.

Our relationship to suffering must change. Although the Buddha did suffer before his enlightenment, he went on to take a huge leap that actually transformed suffering into compassion. Suffering does not automatically create compassion. It is just a tool that can help us to see the larger perspective.

At this time in our evolution, many methods from the past are being communicated and used to facilitate the raising of planetary consciousness. The most profound spiritual secrets that were previously hidden are now readily available for us to explore. Our spiritual moment is now! There is no need to travel far to find a guru. For us to discover all truths, we need only have a strong desire to know.

We now have greater opportunities than ever before to discover the truth of who we are. We must not take this opportunity lightly; rather, we must make it our highest priority. We are at a turning point in our planet's evolution that can either end in destruction or in peaceful coexistence. If we continue to maintain our shortsighted materialistic view of life, destruction may be the scenario. But if we open our hearts to the wisdom within us and use spiritual techniques that help us to see more clearly the truth of who we are, then peace and joy could be the result.

I must state clearly and strongly that the time to choose which path we want to take is now. Suffering has not only distorted our own experience of life, but has almost destroyed our precious environment. Suffering is not just confined to the body anymore; it is also projected out into everything in our world. We have created imbalance in nature through all of our past deeds. This is the reason for the increased frequency of natural disasters occurring on our planet such as floods, fires, and earthquakes. Nature is trying desperately to cleanse itself and release this suffering.

To begin changing our relationship with suffering, we must first change our idea about it. We can no longer view it as being necessary for growth or to connect with God. Because suffering perpetuates suffering, minimizing our own suffering will relieve the suffering of others. You must believe me! I am here to serve you and to raise your consciousness so that you may see more clearly. You are here to live in *total joy*, not to suffer. This is humanity's true destiny.

Beloved Blessings

Blessings come in many forms, such as: "God bless you," "You have been blessed," "It's a blessing in disguise," and "Bless her little heart." To bless is to connect and join with the one we are blessing. The act of blessing is not just restricted to priests, ministers, and rabbis. It is a spiritual act that anyone can participate in to wish someone or something well.

We need to perform this sacred act more often. Blessing is our innate tendency to help our fellow sisters and brothers. It is so powerful that it can change a person's life. However, the only way that it will work is if we believe in its power completely. Doubtful people will be unable to focus enough energy to send a blessing that has impact. It will be like an airplane running out of gas before it gets to its destination.

How focused and centered we are in *love* determines how fast results are produced. When a thought arises in the mind, we listen to the thought first and then decide if it's worth focusing on or not. If we decide to forget it, our mind and body cease to produce energy regarding the thought. But if we decide the thought is something that is important to us, the mind will continue to focus on it until it manifests.

To avoid focusing on wrong thoughts that create negativity in our lives, we must scrutinize our thoughts. We must realize that we have a choice. If we don't allow a negative thought that enters our mind to linger, it will dissipate quickly. But if we allow it to continue to engage our mind, we will begin to manifest it. And once the mind has manifested such a thought in physical form, it is harder to dispel.

Blessings work the same way. When a positive intention (a blessing) is being felt in the heart, the mind begins to project this feeling outward. Energetically, the person being blessed receives this blessing. The intensity of focus on the blessing determines the potency of the energy received. This is why believing in ourselves is so important.

If we believe that our mental, spiritual, and physical powers can work together to create a bond of love, this bond has no limits. The problem is that our mind, body, and spirit are rarely in unison. They are constantly battling each other and creating much chaos in our lives. If we used our hearts to determine what we want from life, our mind and body would follow. But our heart is usually the last thing we listen to. Instead, we use only our mind or our body to guide us. Our mind can rationalize changing truths into lies and vice versa, while our body often wants only physical gratification and can choose comfort over truth. It's our heart that always knows the truth and has the capacity to bring forth the message of our soul. If we listen to our heart, we won't dismiss truth because it seems too scary, too risky, and too unknown. If we would reclaim our heart as the wisest, most precious, and most knowledgeable aspect of who we are, our lives would begin to run more smoothly. We create a pyramid of power that is unbeatable when we listen to the heart, interpret with the mind, and manifest through the body.

It is this power that makes a blessing manifest. The desire to help others strengthens the bonds we have with them. The more we connect with others, the bigger the pyramid becomes. Indeed, we create a new existence for mankind through the act of offering blessings. Compassionately blessing family, friends, strangers, and even enemies, brings the realization that we ourselves are blessed to have each and every one of them in our lives.

We must go beyond feeling competition and jealousy towards others because that energy returns to us and causes us never to be satisfied. We must be aware that our own uncharitable thoughts towards others will eventually affect us negatively. For example, when we hear that another is suffering and we think, "I'm glad it's him and not me," we are actually being self-destructive. Inevitably, one day we will be the one suffering and there will be no one to wish us well. What we put out comes back to us “ten fold.” We must make a mental note that the next time such thoughts arise in our mind we will not accept them anymore. Instead, we will give the suffering person a blessing, truly wishing that his or her pain would go away.

Such actions can pull us out of the depths of despair and elevate us. In wanting the best for everyone, we more easily receive the best for ourselves. Therefore, we must open our hearts and let love flow out to every living thing. In reality, because there is no separation between us and them, by blessing others in an unselfish way, we are blessing ourselves. Our compassion for others automatically returns to us and, interestingly, this is where *self-love* can begin. This is easily recognizable from the happiness we receive each time we help another.

Let blessings be a new way for us to greet others. In saying hello, we can project a thought such as, "I want only the best for you because you deserve it." Let's truly understand the meaning of the Golden Rule that says, "Do unto others as you would have done unto you." In other words, only do to others what you would like done to yourself. Only when this is achieved on a fundamental level will suffering be eliminated on this planet.

Feeding the Soul rather than Counting Calories

Society is obsessed with counting calories. This obsession moves beyond our relationship with food to the core of how we relate to ourselves. The saying, "You are what you eat," is true to a certain extent, on the physical level. But on a deeper level, the real question is, "How well do we really know ourselves?"

Food was provided by God to give us the energy we need to empower our minds and bodies. We rarely use it for this purpose, however, so the calories we take in often become fat. Consequently, many people are overweight. The desire to overeat has nothing to do with hunger, but comes from a sense of inadequacy that stems from one feeling fragmented rather than whole. It is similar to completing only half of a puzzle without being able to find the rest of the pieces to complete it. We try in every physical way possible to fill these empty spaces. Overeating or under eating has become a common attempt at filling this void.

Another modern day problem is that our choices of food have also deteriorated. We often eat food now that can actually harm us instead of making healthier choices of food that would nurture and support our physical well being. All of these dysfunctional behaviors are a reflection of the lack of love and respect we have for ourselves.

Many times our self concepts are low because we cannot fulfill the expectations that have been placed on us by parents, school, society, and to a great extent, ourselves. Since we will never be the perfect person we dream of being, we punish ourselves by indulging our bodies with many different harmful substances. These include junk food, drugs, alcohol, and cigarettes.

The fact is, it's not our stomach that is starving, but rather our soul—and not for food, but for *truth*. Such truth can only be found by understanding what's preventing us from feeling satisfied. The deeper we look at our self-defeating sense of inadequacy, the clearer it becomes that this needs to be understood, worked with, and finally let go of. When we are not in touch with ourselves physically, mentally, and spiritually, this leaves a void and makes us susceptible to bad habits. These bad habits temporarily relieve the pain that comes from not knowing who we are. Over-indulgence in *anything* is a clear sign that we are avoiding our real problem. With each new layer of fat comes an additional layer of problems. Without consciously looking at our feelings of inadequacy, these problems and these layers of fat will not go away. However, when self-negation is consciously transformed into self-love, we complete the puzzle and begin to feel whole.

To transform these feelings of inadequacy, we must realize that it's not counting calories that's important. What really matters is counting each one of our beautiful qualities. Everyone *is* born with tremendous potential that we simply need to discover and develop. Our perfection already exists, and the hunger we feel is the hunger to get acquainted with it. Such things as food, money, material objects, and power do not bring us closer to our perfection. Rather, they only create distractions that keep us further away from it. The truth that each of us can connect to our perfection is what I'm here to tell you. Our true food is light, energy and love—the source of all life. Positive thoughts and convictions, dedication, creativity, generosity, wisdom, self-respect, acceptance, compassion, kindness, and awareness are the things that increase the mind's consciousness and create a force that sets us on a path to realizing our perfection, a perfection which feeds our soul.

Rather than only knowing these ideas on an intellectual level, we must allow them to sink in more deeply so that a true shift in awareness can penetrate our being. When this occurs, there isn't any reason for counting calories. Our bodies automatically know what kind and how much food is needed to live a healthy life. We don't need diets. We need only to realize our innate perfection.

Gaining Self-Respect

If we *respect* ourselves, all other beings will respect us too. Our attitude about ourselves determines the responses and attitudes we receive from others. When we respect ourselves, this opens the door to elevated energy and creates an environment of mutual respect. If we have low self-esteem and little respect for ourselves, however, this will promote an environment of diminished respect from others.

Human bodies have a vibration that can be easily detected. This vibration attracts people who have similar vibrations. Since our soul always wants what's best for our personal growth and sees the whole picture, it knows what impact a specific relationship will have on us. Consequently, it is we, ourselves, who decide if we want to learn and grow from a particular relationship or if we want to continue to repeat the same mistakes. We're in charge, and it is we who determine the outcome of our life.

For example, we may continually attract people who abuse us. This is a pattern that will not be broken until we understand the root of the problem and recognize that we do not deserve abuse. This is only the first step, though, because we must then act on this insight or our predicament will remain the same. And even if we leave an abusive partner, we will attract another person who will mistreat us if this change does not reflect a new awareness. The situation will be repeated, over and over, until we realize that this is not the other person's fault and that they are only acting as a mirror for us so that we can see clearly what our underlying issues are. When we are truly able to see this and take responsibility for it, we are then able to change our behavior by bringing the light of consciousness into the situation. The result will be an act of love towards ourselves and towards others.

We must continually work on loving ourselves. To do this, we must acknowledge the beautiful and unique qualities we have and cherish them. We can then draw on these strengths when life becomes difficult.

Each of us is born with unique talents and special qualities. These qualities are our gifts to the world. Our contributions to the world are what help us develop our self-respect. By sharing our strengths, we help others to discover their strengths. This brings us great satisfaction and gives us a sense of self-worth.

We must open the door to our heart. We can then allow this openness to spin a web of connectedness between us in an atmosphere of love and respect. By doing this, we will gain respect for ourselves and for all living things. The two go hand in hand like lovers, like friends, like equals.

Forgiving

What does it take to forgive someone? It might simply take accepting an apology. Or it might take years of resentment followed by therapy. Perhaps it means accepting the fact that an offensive act was necessary in the larger context of life. At any rate, the hurt that we sustain provokes feelings that need to be looked at.

It is important to realize that we actually choose situations unconsciously so that we can see and learn from them. Sometimes, because we do not want to deal with our feelings, we repress them and blame other people or other circumstances for them. It then often follows that we refuse to forgive others and everyone suffers as a result.

When a seemingly unwanted confrontation occurs, both parties have already subconsciously agreed to play their roles in it. Subsequently, both parties have something to learn from it. These difficult situations provide a way of showing us what challenges need to be worked on in our lives. But instead of working through such situations, we often become defensive, attempting to protect ourselves from pain. This keeps us from understanding the underlying issues behind the challenge. Unfortunately, our shields do not help us progress. Instead, they cause us to remain angry and unforgiving.

We must open our minds to the fact that there are reasons for everything that happens in life. Being the recipient of disrespectful and degrading behavior can make us feel like a victim. In reality, though, *nobody is a victim*. Instead of immediately feeling victimized, we must ask ourselves what it is that we might need to learn from a situation that angers us. For every person the lesson is different. While one individual may need to learn more self-respect, another may need to learn to admit they are wrong.

The anger one feels following a painful experience needs to be confronted. If it's not, it will eventually cause illness. Awareness that an action resulting in anger happened with our unconscious consent is the first step toward healing. You may wonder how anything as negative as being raped could be an unconscious choice. Although to our rational mind such a choice does not make sense, we must see that even though we only want positive things to happen in our life, there would be no reason for introspection and change if only positive things took place. If we were perfect, negative situations would never need to occur. But since we are not perfect, our soul plans events that seem terrible to us in order to help us wake up from unconsciousness.

We must have *faith* that our soul knows what is best for us. It is our connection to God and the truth. Many people in our society do not see that the negative things which occur in life could actually be blessings in disguise and that conflicts may arise when the soul selects difficult situations for us. So instead of looking at the underlying issues brought up by such situations, we usually try to avoid them in every way possible. When we feel hurt and angry, we either punish ourselves or blame others. Instead, we must change this negative pattern by humbly forgiving them and ourselves and looking deeply at the lessons to be learned from the situation.

When we realize that we are in a dangerous or unhealthy situation, we must have enough self-respect and courage to leave it. If it's too difficult to leave the situation on our own, we need to get help from those we know who will give us the necessary support and love. And if we see that it is a child who is being abused, or anyone who is too small and afraid to protect his or herself, it is the duty of a parent, sibling, or neighbor to intervene. We must all participate in each other's well being and have a sincere concern for one another.

Ultimately, it is important to remember that we are not victims in life, even though we often feel this way. We feel this way because we have lost our self-love and our love for others. A way to reconnect with this love is to forgive—both ourselves and others. By creating a lightness in our hearts and bodies, we facilitate a healthy life and happiness for all.

Intuition as Divine Communication

What can we say about our intuition? Is it vivid or is it vague? Is it important or is it ignored? Is it heard or is it silent? Is it developed or is it immature? How often do we listen to our intuition?

Intuition, a powerful "sense of knowing," is an instrument of our soul to discover the truth. Our mind questions and analyzes, but many times it is influenced by outside factors that then distort our perceptions. Our emotions also contribute to our decision-making, but these, too, can irrationally alter our perspective. Although our mind and emotions play an important role in our lives, they can also be misleading when used for the purpose of discovering what's true and for making decisions.

Unlike our mind and emotions, our intuition comes from a deeper level of wisdom, a level at which only truth exists. This enables us to make wise choices. It's our heart and soul, working together, that gives us this innate knowing. Moreover, our intuition can be developed to the point where every choice we make is based on it. Numerous times a day we automatically use our intuition, quite naturally, without even thinking about it. However, when an important decision has to be made, we tend to forget this "fountain of wisdom." We begin to assess the problem mentally or emotionally, or ask the advice of family and friends, which often just creates further confusion and distress. If we never use our intuition, we may even begin to lose the ability to hear it. This lack of confidence in our own innate knowing is pervasive in our culture. We no longer trust in our own wisdom and feel we must look for answers elsewhere. We can change the old patterns, however, by realizing that we actually have all the answers within us. Even though few people know or remember how to access this place of wisdom, and many believe it is unattainable, this is not the case.

Our first reaction to something is usually based on our intuition. Soon, however, our mind starts to interfere and our emotions get involved. This is when we need to stop and take time to *relive* our first impression. We must probe more deeply, not with our mind or our emotions, but with our intuitive knowing. When we reach a place that feels right and natural, this is that place of intuition, the place of truth. We need to pay attention to how this place feels so that the next time it will be easier to locate. Silence is an important avenue to intuition, for only a still mind can find this place. Therefore, doing things such as taking walks in nature, gardening, meditating, or just slowing down in general will help us to access this small, but powerful, voice of our soul.

Could there be anything more important than learning to feel and know what's true for us? Our intuition is God's way of communicating with us, making the truth always available. Relying on our intuition brings a wonderful feeling of connection. It makes us aware of our connection to Self and to all humankind. In turn, this makes our choices in life easier. Life then becomes filled with peace and wisdom, the way it was meant to be.

Living in Simplicity

Simplicity is the spice of life, but few people in our culture live simply these days. Simplicity allows us to see the bigger picture and creates balance and serenity in our lives. Unfortunately, we forget that our lives can actually be lived in an uncomplicated way. Our forefathers lived simply and this choice is also ours. But instead of following in their footsteps, we have strived to live in more progressive ways, ways that have provided us with more convenience and comfort, but at the cost of losing our peace of mind.

Simplicity and solitude, qualities of life that were once important, have been largely lost. They have been replaced by the desire for wealth and prestige. We have felt pressured into keeping up with our neighbor's success and, as a result, have become workaholics. As a culture, this way of life has taken a toll on us and many of us now suffer from ailments that are stress related. Living in this manner is unhealthy and must be changed.

A large number of people today *are* beginning to seek an alternative lifestyle. Many people, unhappy with their busy and meaningless lives, are finally saying, "No more. I have a choice, and I will no longer accept money and materialism as my God."

What is this alternative way? The simple way: having enough things to be comfortable, but not so many things that they create burden and debt. It's about choosing a lifestyle that assures time to enjoy the beauty of nature, time to care for each other, and time for quietness and solitude. This solitude is essential to maintain a healthy body and mind. It is our connection to God and to our spiritual lives.

Without setting time aside each day for keeping such a connection, our world begins to collapse. People begin showing symptoms of anxiety and depression. To remain healthy, we must start thinking for ourselves and avoid mass media pressures. We must create our own lives, following our dreams and aspirations. Society and the media have conditioned us to believe that we can't live happily without an over abundance of material things. But this way of thinking is limiting our ability to take charge of our lives. We must now realize that this is a form of brainwashing which is subliminally controlling our ideas and decisions. One of God's greatest gifts to us is *free will*. Have the courage to reclaim that gift, because only this can help us follow our hearts and find our own true path.

Each of you has a special talent to share with the world. What is yours? You should experiment to find this talent and then share it generously. Doing what you love to do is what makes life meaningful and joyful. Working at a job you dislike, just to pay bills and buy excessive possessions, creates a life devoid of meaning. Without true meaning in life, our souls feel empty and lost, creating despair. This despair is talking to us, saying, "It's time to change your existence. Don't you hear your soul calling you? Please do not waste any more precious time, for as soon as you begin to do what you love, I'll no longer bother you."

Here is the encouragement, dear ones, that you've been waiting for: I see each one of you as you read this and I bestow upon you a blessing of clarity and courage. It will help you to change the course of your life. So go *now* and make your mark upon life's destiny, for your individual life is indispensable to the whole of life. Know this and rejoice in it!

Hell on Earth

Does hell really exist or is it something made up to frighten us and to keep us from sinning? Is there really even such a thing as a sin? Is it possible that we go through life fearing things that just don't exist? In contrast to the notion of hell, most people who have physically died and returned to life say that they have experienced a beautiful place where a feeling of love and peace prevails. How do we make sense of this?

To better understand how the concept of hell developed, let's first imagine a group of people, elected by the government, whose duty is to keep peace in their province. One of the first things they would do is to make up rules for people to abide by and designate punishment for people who disobeyed them. To assure further obedience, they would instill fear by devising a place where those who disobeyed would be sent—a jail or prison.

Similarly, religion had to find a system that would frighten the masses into behaving the desired way. It is for this purpose that hell was created. If anyone disobeyed the laws of religion, they would be considered a "sinner" and would be punished in the afterlife by going to hell. Hell was depicted as an evil place where the devil presided in the presence of fire. In actuality, hell is a superstition created to terrify people into obeying religious laws.

Another belief created by religion is that God persecutes those who do not obey his rules. Actually, God always treats every living entity as he would treat himself—with love and kindness. God's judgment of others was invented by various religions to influence the behavior of humankind. Unfortunately, this has not helped our race; it has only instilled fear and anxiety within us. We have become puppets, living our lives by rules and fears created by our governments and churches. This is not God's way; God does not judge.

God gives everyone the choice to decide how they want to live their life. Is a mistake a sin or could it be more like a child who innocently tries many paths to see what works? Our so-called "sins" are actually experiences that create our personal identity and help us to grow. These experiences need to be cherished instead of condemned because they show us the direction we need to take. God is loving and full of compassion. He *wants* us to discover our own path in life.

Knowing this, we need to reassess all that we've been taught to fear in order to see mistakes as lessons and opportunities for transformation. Our acceptance of guilt and suffering are unnatural and unnecessary—*they* create a "hell" for us right here on earth. We must no longer accept such lies; instead, we must open our hearts and feel that God is only love and nothing more.

We are here to experience life to its fullest and nothing should compromise this. We must learn to accept all of ourselves fully. This means that we must not only accept our good qualities, but also our weaknesses. It is we who judge ourselves, not God. God understands that if something is not working in our lives it's time to change it. God also knows that we often have trouble doing this. Our desire for security is actually what keeps our unconscious habits going and keeps us from trying anything new. But this is too high a price to pay. We must now intuit which rules were made by man and which ones were made by God. Then we must discontinue obeying the man-made rules that kill the human spirit. We must individually make our own laws based upon our own particular relationship with God. These laws will differ for every being because each has a unique relationship with God.

Hell exists as a result of our inability to honor life and honor God. When we forget to see the perfection in everything, this is hell. When we dwell on our problems without hope, this is hell. When we allow poverty to continue without lending a helping hand, this is hell. When we pollute nature, this is hell. When we ignore and resist all signs for change, this is hell. And when our hate, anger, and negativity dominate our lives, this is hell. Despite what society and religion say, our hell is created right here on earth, and only here.

Religions have created an image of hell in the afterlife to make us fearful so that we will give over our power to them. But God does not want us to hand over our power; rather, God is asking us to live a life in which all is accepted, including every perfection *and* every mistake—because without mistakes, there would not be perfection.

If we resist change in our lives, we actually create hell for ourselves. We do this by unconsciously choosing to live in a state of stagnation, ignorance, and conformity rather than love. Since God is always with us, we should not fear taking this leap of faith. It is a leap that is preparing us for "heaven on earth," not hell on earth. Have the courage to choose to live in Heaven instead of Hell—*it's all up to you.*

Softness and Transformation

Relaxing into *softness* is what allows our bodies to transform. Our physical body is a storehouse for everything we feel, be it from the mind, body, or soul. Our body does not have the capability to decipher where these feelings are coming from, only the ability to store sensations like a memory bank. Our body digests every thought we think and every emotion we feel.

When we eat, our body digests food and is nourished by the vitamins and minerals in it that keep us healthy. Someone who is aware that the body needs certain elements to stay fit will choose foods that are healthy. If they are unaware of this, they might largely consume unhealthy fast foods. Over time, this will likely cause them to become ill. The illness could then serve as a wake up call to change. Or the cause of the illness could be ignored, reinforcing the belief that the illness was brought on by something over which there is no control.

Just like food, our thoughts and feelings either nourish us or deplete us, depending on whether they are positive or negative. Therefore, our thoughts should also be chosen very carefully before they are stored in the body. If negative thoughts are continually selected, the body will most likely become sick.

When feeling sick, most people will receive medicine from the doctor. The medicine may work for a time, but sooner or later the symptoms will return if one's habits haven't changed. The root of the problem must be found or there will be no real healing.

Because sickness is physical, we tend to believe that it needs to be cured with something physical. But what we really need is to release the tension from the affected areas, creating a soft area. Once such areas are softened, they become vulnerable and open to the real cause of the illness. The memories, fears, and hurts that are the true roots of the illness begin to reveal themselves.

Here are some things that you can do to help the healing process along:

First, before any transformation can occur, you must want to change.

Second, you must take responsibility for your own body and realize that you cannot rely on doctors for a quick cure. Instead, you must dedicate yourself to your total health. There is no room for blaming others; it's time to forgive them and yourself.

Third, you must learn to breathe deeply. This puts space around pain and breaks up any hardness. Put your hands on the area that hurts and give yourself tender loving care. Only loving yourself can bring about softness. Because most people feel undeserving of love, they cannot do this to themselves. They need someone close to them or a professional to help them feel loved.

Fourth, to balance the energy in a blocked part of the body, learn visualizations that aid healing. For example, visualize a metal wall where the sickness is and see it collapsing. Replace this wall with bright sunlight, the light of healing. Let this light penetrate the area. If a sound or tone comes to you, breathe deeply and let this sound out. Repeat this a few times.

Obtaining softness can either be arduous work or a quick transformational process, depending on how ready we are for change. Once softness is felt, it will lead us to the core of the problem, revealing the real reason for the pain. Often it takes an open heart and mind to accept the cause. For example, if an aching back says, "I'm in pain from self-hate," we must be ready to accept the reason and work on loving our selves.

The ability to heal ourselves is innate in every one of us. We long to feel healthy and whole. We were born whole and that is our natural state of being. Because of life's trials and tribulations, we sometimes forget our natural state and can feel fragmented and small. To regain our natural sense of wholeness, we must respond to ourselves and to life with softness. Only when we are soft and vulnerable is it possible to forgive and love ourselves. This is what brings us back to our natural state of wholeness. We can then live life as we were meant to—as healthy, loving, and whole beings.

Justifying and Judging

Why is it that we spend so much of our life justifying our ideas and opinions? Is it because we want to change the minds of others so that they agree with us? Is it that we need their confirmation as proof that we are right? Not confident with our own mind's rationale, it becomes very important for us to be right. To reinforce our perspective, we want others to think the same as we do. The experiences and wisdom we have gained from life are not enough to ensure that we know the truth. Why is this?

Although our paths can run parallel and may even cross each other, each person's development is unique and everyone's reality is different. We might desire that their reality is the same as ours, because of the sense of security that conformity brings and because being different seems lonely and uncomfortable. However, it is not our right to try and change anybody else's ideas. We only have the right to speak from our own perspective and to state our own point of view.

Our judgments create a great separation from one another when we do not accept and respect the distinct reality of others. Judging only reflects our own ignorance, lack of self-confidence, and awareness. By belittling our brothers and sisters, we are inadvertently belittling ourselves. This is because our connection to every living thing is part of our connection to God. So when we diminish another through our prejudice and discrimination, we diminish ourselves. This makes it harder for us to achieve our goals of health, happiness, and peace of mind.

Remember: *God does not judge.* He accepts everyone whether they are white, black, or brown; whether they are rich, poor, smart or ignorant; whether they are Catholic, Buddhist, Muslim, Hindu, Jewish, or atheist. This is because we were all created with infinite possibilities. If only one way was the right way, God would have created everyone the same. But God loves and respects the uniqueness of all individuals. So let's follow in God's footsteps and respect each and every thing alive.

Although the paths of others may be different from our own, they too are children of God; thus, they are our equal. We must rise above petty opinions and feel the energy that binds each one of us together. In the realm in which I live, separateness and differences do not exist. What does exist is the love of God. This all-inclusive love joins us in our love for each other. Don't wait until you die to experience this paradise! You can begin to achieve it here on earth now. God meant life to be this way.

A Helping Hand

Where is your hand when someone needs help . . .
is it in your pocket or is it extended out?

Is it a hand that is warm, soft, and open . . .
or is it a hand that is cold, hard, and closed?

Is it a hand that responds easily to an emergency . . .
or is it a hand that stiffens from the fear of obligation?

Is it a hand that welcomes and enjoys a handshake . . .
or is it a hand that pulls back in fear of human contact?

Is it a hand that moves confidently with expression . . .
or is it a hand that hangs limply with insecurity or indifference?

Is it a competitive hand, pushing when someone else is ahead . . .
or is it a just hand, patient and willing to be fair?

Is it a hand that hits when it is mad . . .
or is it an attentive hand, tolerant to all opinions?

Our hands are the physical expression of who we really are, deep down inside. We can fool ourselves with our minds into believing that we are caring, loving, and open, but if we watch our hands, the truth will be revealed. So tell me:

Where is your hand when someone needs help . . .
is it in your pocket, or is it extended out?

Patience as Therapy

Patience has always been considered a very important virtue. Indeed, it is even more important than we think. Patience is the most calming therapy that exists; it gives us time to appreciate the details in life and it enables us to see the larger picture of life. It reveals to us that our busy lifestyles often create stress and can be unhealthy and dangerous. Patience grabs us by the hand and takes us for a walk—it sets the pace of our steps, ensuring that we are able to receive the fullness of each moment.

By contrast, impatience causes us to interfere with nature's cycle, pushing us too fast and altering our natural course. We live in a society where instant results, instant gratification, and instant feedback control us. We no longer have the sense that our lives should consist of both movement and stillness. Thus, we have no time to put both of our feet on the ground, causing us to lose our balance and stability. This imbalance makes us feel impatient and frustrated, which can easily turn into negative action. This sets a poor example for our children who no longer know the meaning of patience. Consequently, the balance of nature and our own equilibrium have suffered, causing a downward spiral of turmoil and distress in the world.

Let's take the time to relearn the virtue of patience. Having patience has many benefits. It aids us when learning new job skills, getting over an illness, waiting in line, finishing a project, and it even opens the way to the fulfillment of dreams. Let's calm down and be willing to wait for the right moments to "seize the opportunities" that will contribute to our growth and happiness. It is our patience that helps us to reflect before making decisions and it is our patience that aids us in reaching our goals. Patience guides us and keeps us in touch with the rhythm of life. Let's embrace our patience and allow it to come forth so that we can find our true path and regain our priceless and precious peace of mind.

Giving Graciously

Many within our society have lost the capacity to give graciously. Our giving often comes from a sense of obligation rather than from the heart. Many times the more wealth a person, group, or country has, the more it holds onto it. Why is this? We place much more importance on the material world than on the spiritual realm. We are insecure and we fear that our wealth may disappear at any moment. We usually worry about ourselves first, our family next, and our friends and others after that. We accept the teachings that it is not our duty to help everyone and therefore we rarely think about the starving people living around the world. We believe that our responsibilities lie only with ourselves and with our family.

This is not true. Our actual responsibilities include all human beings and all living things. Since we are all connected, we all suffer—even if unconsciously—if only one person suffers in the world. This cannot continue. We must face our responsibility for our brothers and sisters across the globe and help to change the world condition.

We might think that this is too much responsibility, but this, too, is not true. We don't need to help every person, face-to-face. But we do need to feel connectedness and compassion for the less fortunate living on earth. Seeing ourselves in their predicament will automatically cause us to feel connected and compassionate toward them. What if we were living in Africa sick with AIDS or starving to death? Wouldn't we appreciate help on any level?

Compassion comes from an open heart. When we meet unfortunate people or see them on television, we should look at them deeply and try to understand what they are going through. It's not just a bad day at work for them—it's their life "unraveling at the seams." For example, consider the mother who escapes a flood by staying five days in a tree with her seven children. Finally, a helicopter rescues the family. Caught in their position, we would probably pray that someone is compassionate enough to appreciate our plight and realize that help is needed. It's not important how we help, or how much or little we help, or whether we give money, fly a helicopter, or say a prayer. What really matters is that we incorporate the act of giving into our lives and that we are truly concerned for the well being of humanity.

Let's not sit back in our easy chairs and become oblivious or lazy to life's challenges. Sure, there's time to watch a football game, but we must also take time for charity and kind thoughts. Moreover, it doesn't matter if the needy are red, black, yellow, or white; everyone has a heart and everyone feels. Often our kindness is lost in our discrimination of color, status, and religion. But our brothers and sisters in all areas of the world need us, so our compassion must encompass all people.

Giving is a spiritual act of love that comes back to us full circle—the more we give, the more we receive—on all levels of life. Generosity opens us up to receiving greater abundance in all aspects of our lives. Responding with compassion to others may seem overwhelming at first, but once we give, we soon realize how rewarding giving is and that our lives can change enormously for the better. In fact, we learn that gracious giving is one of our best qualities. This is because we see that if we were to live without graciousness, giving would not exist and nobody, not even ourselves, would reap its benefits. So let's open our hearts, open our hands, and open our pocketbooks. Let's learn the meaning of compassion. Our full appreciation of its meaning will initiate our greatest acts of generosity and bring immense contentment and meaning to our lives.

Sacred Sacrifice

Sacrifice is a word that few people like to hear. To most people, it signifies something they must do without or a lack of something. However, sacrifice in the past was considered a great virtue. To sacrifice something meant to *transcend* one's attachment to it. People knew that having the strength to let go of something opened up the possibility of gaining something else. Sacrificing to them was a sacred act of courage and trust because they were giving up something known to acquire something unknown.

Our attachments, which are an important aspect of our physical existence, are not easy to let go of. What would happen if we just said one morning, "I am leaving my home, my work, and my circumstances in search of something more meaningful?" Most people would think this too great a sacrifice and would wonder if this objective could be achieved without such drastic measures. But altering one's circumstances can allow change to happen more quickly.

One may sacrifice significant tangible things like a house, a job, or even a marriage to attain much needed intangible things that are also significant, such as a less stressful life or the pursuit of happiness. Since material reality is important to most people, this sacrifice could appear to be a huge loss. When we look at the larger picture, however, we realize that gaining valuable things such as love, peace, and joy are more important than keeping careers, relationships, or material objects that may be void of these qualities. Sometimes we do not need to sacrifice one to get the other, but other times, by letting go of something first, space is created for something else to enter.

Sometimes, by simply changing our attitude and becoming more open and accepting of what is, our situation will change without having to sacrifice anything. Our ability to shift our perception enables us to see the same subject in a completely different way. For example, we may have always hated the color red, but one morning we wake up loving the color red. Why such a change? Maybe red symbolized a moment in the past that caused us pain. If we shift our perception by giving up and transcending that moment of pain, the color red can be instantly transformed into a color that now gives us warmth and pleasure.

Transforming our perceptions may seem like a simple feat. In reality, however, it is not simple at all for most of us. This is because we can be afraid to change *anything*, even an address, much less a perception. We are conditioned to live life very much the same way as we lived it when we were children. And because many of us lived in dysfunctional environments when we were young, our lives were drained of much of its energy. We didn't have the strength to improve our life, so we barely stayed afloat and "treaded water" to keep from drowning. As adults, we are still looking through the same stained glasses we wore as children.

Now it's time to take off those glasses and perceive life in a new way. Such a shift in perception doesn't have to be difficult—it can be as easy as taking off our glasses. We may find that it is our stained glasses that have been blinding our true perception of life, so let's take those glasses off and clearly see our life. Actually, illusions come from the mind, not the eyes.

If there were glasses to correct our mind's illusions, how easy life would be! Unfortunately, such glasses do not exist. Consequently, we must be *clear-sighted* enough without the glasses to see where our mind's perceptions need correction. Once identified, we must then sacrifice the part of ourselves that is living in a blurry world, the part that is blinded by false ideas and misperceptions from the past. We must ask ourselves, "What part of my life should I sacrifice in order to be whole again? What part of my life is an illusion that I can let go of now?" The answer to these questions is usually the part that just isn't working anymore in our lives.

Change requires courage, courage requires initiative, and initiative requires the proper attitude toward sacrifice. We must have the courage to take the initiative to sacrifice, not for others as we think Jesus did, but rather for ourselves, so that we truly become more like Christ.

Living in Different Dimensions

It's not easy for us to comprehend that we live in many different dimensions at one time, incorporating all we have been in the past, will be in the future, and are now. If someone from the beginning of time decided to film and document our existence, they would see that we live many lives simultaneously, with memories that can be drawn on by the subconscious, giving us a warehouse of stored information. It's like a computer programmed to keep all processed data so when information is needed it can be accessed immediately.

This information that is gathered from repeated experiences—basically from our all-knowing wisdom—is our best teacher. It gives us profound insights. Our intuition is activated at just the right moment and says, "I've done this before and I know what to do." What we must remember, however, is to trust and draw from this wisdom. We need to do this rather than look outside ourselves for the answers or to not ask the questions at all for fear of not finding the answer. Unfortunately, lessons we are meant to learn are often overlooked and we repeat our mistakes over and over. Our lives begin to look tragically like a movie stuck on replay. Only by acknowledging, deeply reflecting upon, and accepting our errors and the underlying issues that create them, will we have the possibility to transform them.

Our multidimensional intuitive self can share wisdom, but only if it's asked for. If the computer is not switched on, the screen remains blank. Our desire to know the data is what automatically brings forth the information. Moreover, the blueprint we carry within our cells gives us availability to all knowledge and wisdom. Like the computer and the Internet, we are merely externally duplicating what we already have internally. We need only to click into our own web site of tremendous experiences and wisdom to access and act upon the truth at every moment.

If we could see the computer as a mirror of our own inner workings, it would be a tremendous tool to awaken humanity. Although computers have great potential in helping us to uncover the truth, many are now used to escape the in-line connection we have to our source of wisdom. We must begin to see computers in a bigger way. They are actually a metaphor for us to see and discover that the truth resides within each of us.

Our attitude of looking outside ourselves for the truth, rather than looking within ourselves, is postponing our psychological and spiritual growth while it is excelling our technological progress. By understanding the deeper meaning of our new technology and what it actually represents psychologically and spiritually, we can begin to understand that there is no separation between the mundane and the ultimate—*all* is spiritual and all is working to help us attain the truth of all beings.

Let's open our hearts and our minds to the many dimensions we're able to access. Let's begin to see them as all working together to help raise consciousness. One dimension is neither better nor worse than another. Each is important to show us what truth is in many different ways. So let's follow our intuition and not be afraid to speak our own version of the truth. It only takes a few to live this way and then others will join, like the domino effect. Where this will go we can only imagine.

Life's Struggles

What makes life such a struggle? It's the resistance we have toward change: change of mind, change of heart, change of the physical body, change of work, change of partners, change of ideas, and change of perceptions. Changes we are naturally meant to experience are resisted, causing us to feel stifled and unfulfilled. Without change, however, there is no movement to stimulate our senses and creativity. Still, we often choose security over change, even though it makes us struggle each morning to get up, perhaps to face another boring day with a job we've had for twenty-five years. But we struggle on, daydreaming of winning the lottery or of meeting our prince charming.

We have become creatures of habit, afraid of what's around the next corner. We have lost our sense of adventure and exploration, senses that we need to rediscover. Our world has become so challenging that it's hard to gain the courage necessary to take risks and live life fully. We think twice before making a single move. We are bombarded with media scare, with violence, and with loved ones fearing for our safety. In spite of all this, we must still pursue our dreams.

Our potential must be pushed to its highest level of performance. We must tap into our reserve, spark the ignition, and put our gear into four-wheel drive. We must get up, put the music on, and dance out the door. We have committed ourselves to a brave new world, a world of the 21st century, a world that is alive and kicking. Let's have the courage to make it happen, to take those risks that we've been afraid to take, to aspire to our highest goals, to be so aware that nothing goes unseen, to be so clear that we act before our thought has finished, to be so motivated by our true essence that only good deeds shine through, to feel so inspired that only truth prevails, to open our heart so much that only love is felt, and to connect so deeply with God that trust rather than fear is our guide. This is what we all *should* look forward to and what we all are *capable* of experiencing.

The excitement is in the air and the energy is circling like a Sufi dancer in motion. So stomp your feet and rejoice for what's in store for you. It's a century no soul wants to miss. And you are the ones who are able to witness and celebrate this higher consciousness coming to light and to experience what no one has ever experienced before. Are you ready? Then get set, and go! Don't be left behind. Throw your struggles out the door because you don't need them anymore. The time is now to fulfill your aspirations, your dreams, and your destiny.

I wish you courage, determination, and a great time. Enjoy your Self!

Grandmother Moon

It's Grandmother Moon who's calling us now, and she is saying,
"Look at me and feel me,
for I am here to be seen and here to be felt.

My brilliance and my radiance are manifested on the ocean
at night when I am full and ever so bright.
The waves and the tides feel my vibes
and talk to me, thanking me
for letting them express themselves so free.

Thank goodness they have not forgotten me.
It's the animal kingdom who appreciates and
cherishes my influence because they know that without me,
they would not be,
for there would not be fertility.

It's the human race, I regret to say,
who has lost its relationship with me and
can't find its way.
It hurts me deeply that I am so ignored,
for I am a precious gift sent from the Lord.

Today let this be a turning point in history;
your lives, your hearts, your souls, must reconnect to
Grandmother Moon and it must be soon,
for it is Grandmother Moon who gives you the equilibrium,
the cycles, to live a balanced life
of less hardship, pain, and strife.
Let Grandmother Moon do her job,
the job she was meant to do.

My arms are open, ready to embrace you,
my shining light is here, ready to guide you."

Facing Fear

Resistance blocks the true nature of things. By resisting fear, we increase its potency. To triumph over fear, we must learn to accept all that life has to offer, including fear itself. We need to see that when something wonderful occurs, it's a gift, and that when something horrible happens, it's also a gift. We must embrace *all* moments rather than only those we like. If we love each moment to the fullest, thinking only of that moment and not what happened or what might have happened, we can overcome the resistance that blocks the true nature of things.

Trusting that God is always with us overcomes fear. Mistrust only causes separation from our creator, making us fearful. A result of this is that we fear death. By opening our hearts to death and inviting it in, death becomes our friend rather than our enemy. By not resisting it, death transforms into an amazing awakening. When we face our fear of death, life surrounds and truly enters our beings so that we are able to know aliveness in its truest sense. With this experience, our fear naturally subsides.

We need to open up to the invisible realms and see the pure magic of existence, for it is here that we find the dimension of acceptance and love. It is time to think less of the body and work with the heart and soul. It is our strong heart and soul that heals us physically, emotionally, mentally, and spiritually. For example, look at me: I am ugly, I am poor, I am without possessions, my teeth are dirty, my robe is full of holes, and I have worn out sandals on my scabbed feet. But I do not feel or see this, because my heart is pounding with eternal love and light and encompasses all of my body. That is what I feel and see. This is the true me.

When we are fearful, we must be open and *really listen* to what the heart has to say. And then we must act upon this knowledge. Honor the fear and let it evaporate away naturally. We must take care of ourselves in the present. If we can do this successfully, our future will unfold in the name of God.

The only way to truly help ourselves and others is to drink the nectar of our true being. It is the nectar that creates life and it is the nectar that shows all who drink it the secrets that have been lost for so long. You can reclaim it now with only a sip. See it there in front of you, in a small golden cup. Pick it up, sip it, and let it penetrate your every cell.

Once the truth is felt with total awareness, transformation occurs. For it to occur more easily, see yourself as a bird flying in the sky experiencing many different things. You'll soon see that:

*You feel connected to all living organisms,

*You feel boundless, knowing that everywhere is home,

*You live in the moment, not thinking of what happened in the past and what might happen in the future,

*You don't think, but automatically *know* how to live by instinct and intuition,

*You sing and express yourself naturally,

*You are social and enjoy flying in flocks, but you also fly alone and take great pleasure and delight in your aloneness,

*If you are attacked, you defend yourself and want to survive,

*You express fear naturally when other birds threaten to hurt you or take your food,

*When you fly, you allow yourself to flow with the air currents without fighting them,

*You mate and have baby birds,

*You feed your babies and lovingly care for them,

*You die not thinking of death but innately knowing that everything is always changing and that your death has a place in this change,

*You accept all that life gives without asking why and without asking how.

A bird lives in a perfect state, moment-to-moment, feeling life through its wings and expressing it with pure instinctive actions. If we could truly live the life of a bird for only one day, our fear would be faced and we would be truly transformed.

Expanding Horizons

It is time to prepare for the coming era of higher consciousness. Together we will join in wisdom and compassion. Awareness will shine throughout this planet. Those of you who sense this are here to help others understand it. As this era approaches, life will not be the same. For many who hold on to the past and are unable to change, it will be devastating.

How can we prepare for this? We are prepared by awakening to the truth of who we really are. And how can we do this? We can do this by living in the moment and seeing deeply into the truth that each moment reveals to us.

When we realize that we are *not* this body/mind and understand that it is only a form that consciousness has created to speak through, then we have a chance to see the truth. The body/mind is only a vehicle to understand the greater truth of who we are. When we see ourselves as only the body/mind, we lose the possibility of realizing the great vastness that we actually are. This truth unfolds in each moment through personal experience and cannot be received through the intellect. The intellect can only point to it.

Although the past has some value in revealing how we arrived at our current situation, and provides us with lessons that help us in the future, dwelling in either the past or the future is a distraction that stops us from living in the moment.

Many people live for the great memories of the past that actually weren't that great. When the present is unfulfilling, we tend to remember a wonderful past. We then hope for a better future, a loving, gratifying, exciting future. But what do we end up with? Only nostalgic memories of how grand the past was and hopeful expectations for the future. But the space of time where actual living takes place is in the present moment.

We are taught that the past holds incredible knowledge. And it does to a point, because it allows us to learn from our mistakes and to gain wisdom from these experiences. But it is essential to examine at what point dwelling in the past becomes harmful. When our thoughts are more than ten percent in the past, our mind is overindulging in occurrences that are no longer important to us. This wastes our energy and gives us a false perception of life.

Living in the present is the greatest gift that we can give ourselves. This gift has been pre-sent to us from God, the Omni-present, in the hopes that we will be in the ever-present at all times. Why is it so important to be in the here and now? It is because people who live in the moment experience life more deeply. They are in harmony with the cycles of life and accept everything that happens, not resisting anything. They are an instrument of consciousness, knowing spontaneously how to respond to everything that comes up in life.

Living in the moment helps alter our perspective of life. This is because life is ever-moving and ever-changing; it is far from being mundane or predictable. So we must learn to be flexible with every new circumstance that arrives. It's like a race car driver who after driving a long straight stretch of highway wants to experience a thrilling curve. If he takes the easy way and chooses the straight course, he may feel secure and even win, but will he feel satisfied? We must feel satisfied with our life in the present. And if we are not, then we must change our course.

Many times our course changes without our approval. We may lose our job, our partner, or our health. These are not accidental. This is our Higher Self, telling us that it's time for a transformation. We must learn to accept life's changes, for only then are we truly living in the moment and only then are we fully immersed and alive. It is only in the present moment that we are free from being manipulated by past memories or future hopes.

In the future, many things will be changing on earth and we must be ready to accept them. Our life is much more than our security and possessions; it's more than our past or future. It is living in the truth, in the moment, in our hearts. It is time to push beyond our boundaries and face each moment as a chance to expand our horizons and to venture into the unknown. It is time to face our fear. We must have the courage to explore new territory, for those who do this will be ready for the new age. Let's not be frightened, for it will be beautiful. Believe me, I would not deceive you. I only wish to inspire you, for *you are of me* and *I am of you*. We are here together, so there is no need to be afraid because I will never leave you.

Seeing the Beauty of Life

The beauty of life cannot be bought, it can only be appreciated. It's like a stained glass window when the sun is shining through it and making bright reflections on the wall. The spectrum of color radiates incredible light, revealing the intricate diversity that exists on this planet.

But how much of this beautiful spectrum do we really see? When our hearts are closed, so are our senses. This makes many aspects of life's beauty invisible to us. We keep our hearts shut down in the hopes of avoiding pain, but the result of closing our hearts is that we live our lives missing the full spectrum of beauty that we were meant to experience.

This beauty is not actually hidden. It can be easily overlooked, though, because we often take for granted what surrounds us. Can you imagine the earth without trees? Would you miss them or would you forget them? What would happen if one morning the sun didn't rise? You wouldn't last a day without its warmth, would you? And how could you live without air to breathe and water to drink? You take these essential elements for granted, forgetting that without any one of them you could not survive. And so it is with everything else that may pass your notice. But everything in life was created in perfect balance by God and has a purpose. He made sure that all living species on earth have what they need to survive and coexist together harmoniously.

Life's beauty must always be consciously *cherished.* When we appreciate and understand deeply the workings of nature, we realize how dependant we are upon nature. Our relationship to nature is like that of a mother and her newborn baby: the child would die if the mother were to disappear. This realization is frightening to most people because we are admitting that we are not self-sufficient and must rely on “outside forces" to keep us alive. But instead of communing with nature and allowing it to nurture us, many of us try to destroy it, yearning for the feeling of power and control over it. Then as beauty turns to ugliness, due to humankind’s so called progress, we simply get used to it and fail to comprehend the magnitude of our loss.

Examples of this can be seen in such man made disasters as the cutting down of millions of trees, air and water pollution, and the extinction of many plant and animal forms, to name only a few. To wage war on nature is to wage war on God. We are destroying nature, which is God's most precious gift. Even though we threaten nature with destructive actions, nature lovingly defends itself from our attacks the best it can, striving to protect the human race.

What will it take to reverse this situation? How may nature's beauty and wholeness be restored and shine through again? Instead of mistreating nature because we want to overpower it, we must learn to embrace and commune with nature in all its magnificence. Life is extraordinarily beautiful in all its forms of expression, and the moment we deeply feel this sacred truth, our existence will be transformed.

Each flower is communicating its essence when it opens its petals, whispering, "Look at my brilliant colors. Smell me. Pick me. I bloom to create beauty in life for all to experience." Animals, too, are devoted to us, despite our often cruel behavior towards them. They teach us to love unconditionally, which is one of the most important lessons of life. The mountains and forests give us inner peace and a place to feel the presence of God. The seasons teach us about the cycles of life, so that we may learn to accept change as a natural process of life. The tides, waves, and streams show us how to flow with life's changes. The sun, the moon, the planets, and the stars shine so that we may learn how to shine within and share our inner light with others. The fruit trees and vegetable plants supply us with nutrients to keep us healthy. The herbs provide us with medicine, so we may be cured when we are ill. The birds sing their music, inspiring us to dance in celebration of our existence. And the air enables us to breathe in the very essence of life and to feel the tremendous energy nature provides us with.

Nature humbly and unconditionally bestows upon us all of her beauty and support. Yet in return, we give thanks by taking nature for granted and destroying it. Instead, we must expand our awareness so that we can see nature as the precious gift that it is from God. We will then be able to deeply express our gratitude to nature. Doing this will prepare the way for healing nature, as well as healing our Selves as a part of nature.

Nature takes care of us and is one hundred per cent devoted to us. It's time we reciprocate by using what she is offering, by thanking her graciously, and by devoting ourselves to her, our generous Mother Nature.

The Grand Finale

Our last talk, I must say, brings tears to my eyes. Of course, my work does not end here. If there is one thing that I wanted to teach, it's that our potential for creativity is *limitless.* Each completion of a project or cycle is just a stepping stone preparing us for the next challenge so that we may continue this process with more experience and wisdom. Even the times when our stagnation, doubts, insecurities, and depression halt us from being creative, it should be regarded as only a break in time to help us re-collect our inner treasures and continue being creative. Our ups and downs jolt us into remaining conscious in everything we do. Do not resist the downs for they are here to serve us in a profound way. Our deepest despair unites with our deepest joy, creating perfection. We must learn more on how to live in this state of perfection.

I do not reveal these messages because I know better or because I am more evolved than you. I went through all that you are going through now. I sincerely know your trials and tribulations and that is why I wanted to write this book. My life was full of doubts, pain, and sickness. I want you to know that such struggles are normal, especially for a saint, since we often take on burdens for which other people are not ready. The one clarity we do have, however, is that we know this pain must be accepted in order to evolve to higher consciousness. I am truly sorry, as is God, for the pain that is so rampant on earth, but I ask you to see it as necessary for movement towards perfection. I humbly admit that this was also not easy for me. Instead of accepting my pain, especially my physical pain, I ignored it and trivialized it, dying at the young age of forty-four. Even though our physical death always occurs at the perfect time for us, I do feel that if I had paid more attention to my physical being, I would have lived longer and thus could have spoken my truths with more people. Instead, I am sharing my messages in this book.

I know some people will doubt that what is written in this book truly came from me, but I ask that if these messages speak to your heart, then listen and learn, because they are truths for you. Our teacher arrives when we are ready. Each one of us has our own path that must be explored. I respect all paths and understand that all paths do lead to the same outcome. It's our preferences and styles that make this difference and not the Essence: the Essence is one and the same.

I want to thank each and every one of you for listening to me. I've tried to make each message as clear and easy as possible for you to grasp, because the simple way has always been my way. If you find discrepancies or disagree with what I say, I full-heartedly understand, for each one of us lives in our own reality.

Be of love, of light, and of Self. Every one of you counts tremendously, in my eyes and in God's eyes. I bless you and am waiting for your friendship. I see and hear every one of you. Confide in me, because I do have the power to help you. Your loving, honest, and sincere wishes are my command.

I bid you farewell for now and await your decision on how you will create your life. It's all in your hands, your dear, dear hands. May love shine through you, around you, and in all that you touch, for there is nothing—*nothing*—more powerful than the power of love.   Your saint, Francis

Cheri's End

I feel sad that this book has come to an end. These last two days in La Verna have been very emotional for me. Spurts of crying, sadness, loss, completion, and joy move in and out of my body, without control. This book has opened up a part of me that I have never known.

My deep commitment to completing it with St. Francis has given me a confidence I have never felt before. The creative power running through my body while I've been channeling this book has amazed me and confirmed for me that we have greater capabilities than we can ever imagine.

The concentration I have acquired through determination and persistence has shown me that we can change. St. Francis's love and guidance has been given to me with such patience that I know now that I must strive for this kind of contact in my relationships with others and myself.

This experience has brought me closer to my realizations, but not near as far as I would like to be. There is still so much more I need to experience and learn. I, too, must re-read what St. Francis has said and practice this in my life.

I hope these messages will bring insight into the many challenges of life and help people to live more joyfully in today's complex world. Even more than this, I hope St. Francis will be used as a catalyst for all to realize the truth of their being.

I feel very happy, satisfied, and privileged to have served both St. Francis and you. I hope some day our paths will meet so we may share in this celebration of life, together.

Your sister, Cheri

About the Author

Cheri Harris, born and raised in California, left the U.S. at the age of eighteen to begin traveling the world. She has lived overseas in places such as Bali, Indonesia (where she co-owned an international export-import business), Amsterdam, Thailand, the Caribbean, and now, Italy.

At the age of twenty-four, Cheri completed her Montessori studies and began teaching children. Later, she studied Thai Massage in Thailand over a period of ten years and received diplomas from seven different schools.

Cheri has resided in Northern Italy for the last eighteen years and speaks fluent Italian. She is a Thai massage therapist and also teaches Thai massage.

Ten years ago, Cheri's life changed drastically after she was contacted by St. Francis. He gave her messages over a period of three years for the book that he wanted to present to the world. This began a new chapter in Cheri's life. She now gratefully sees herself as a communicator, passing information from a great spiritual teacher to those who are ready and willing to hear these truths. Her highest dedication is to St. Francis and his mission, which is to make all of us more aware of our essential nature and our limitless potential.

Cheri is now leading spiritual tours in Italy to St. Francis's most beloved places.

For more information visit: www.followsaintfrancis.com.

ALSO AVAILABLE FROM SUMMERLAND PUBLISHING

Bringing you books to help make the world a better place.

Jolinda Pizzirani, author of "Soul Survivor," "Inspirations," and "Psychic Princess," now brings us this unique collection of messages directly from the angels for all of us to ponder. Every physical entity can hear angel words, but as a prerequisite they must be open to receiving these messages and of a nature to handle and share them properly. Therefore, Jolinda is merely the transcriptionist in this endeavor, and it is hoped that the material provided within "angel words" will begin to satisfy the hunger you have within you for the many unknown factors abundant in Heaven and on Earth.

"angel words" presents a discussion of subjects suggested by the angels themselves, and in addition answers questions submitted by interested individuals living on Earth today. Future editions of "angel words" will embrace the questions put forth by the readers of this first book, and we will continue until all uncertainties have been calmed. Perhaps, as we travel this journey together, we may begin to more successfully navigate the path that lies ahead.

U. S. $14.95 / CAN $19.95 ISBN: 978-0-9794585-3-8

We all possess the tools we need to direct our lives toward our maximum potential of fulfillment. Sometimes we just need a little reminder.

"How to Live An Exotic Life in an Ordinary World" is just that reminder. In a delightful, friendly style, Michele A Pike invites you to explore and experience the joy of being your unique, exotic self.

Whether its learning to belly dance, whipping up an aromatic Indian dish, treating yourself in a pampering exercise or creating a mystical tent, you are entreated to try new, fun things. Interspersed with these freeing experiments are short inspirations to encourage you when you need it most: what to do if you feel depressed, how to treat a common cold, and how to transform your greatest disappointments into your most profound victories. Whimsical drawings throughout the text help you smile as you grow.

Hidden in these lighthearted explorations are real, significant lessons in letting go of our self-imposed limits and freeing ourselves to enjoy our current lives in all their richness. Enjoy your Exotic Life!

$14.95 US/$19.95 CAN ISBN: 978-0-9794585-4-5

You May Order These Great Books from:
www.summerlandpublishing.com, www.barnesandnoble.com, www.amazon.com
Or find them in your local bookstore or gift shop!